What The Bible Says About Purpose

David Ramos

Copyright © 2017 by David Ramos.

ALL RIGHTS RESERVED.

No part of this publication may be reproduced, distributed, or transmitted in any form or by any means, including photocopying, recording, or other electronic or mechanical methods, without the prior written permission of the publisher, except in the case of brief quotations embodied in critical reviews and certain other noncommercial uses permitted by copyright law. For permission requests, please contact the author through the Contact Form on his website: RamosAuthor.com

All Scripture quotations, unless otherwise indicated, are taken from the Holy Bible, New International Version®, NIV®. Copyright ©1973, 1978, 1984, 2011 by Biblica, Inc.™ Used by permission of Zondervan. All rights reserved worldwide.
www.zondervan.com The "NIV" and "New International Version" are trademarks registered in the United States Patent and Trademark Office by Biblica, Inc.™

Thank you!

Congratulations on picking up this book and taking the next step on your journey of purpose. You are one of the few who are taking god's call upon your life seriously. As a thank you, I've also created a free guide titled "5 Questions That Create Clarity" that will give you the tools you need to go even further.

To claim your free copy simply go to http://www.ramosauthor.com/clarity-questions.

Introduction

If you're reading this, chances are you know what frustration feels like. You would describe yourself as a person of faith, of trust, and even of ambition. But for all the work and energy you've poured into your life, you still find yourself hitting walls. Big brick roadblocks keeping you from the thing you're meant to do.

I've been where you are. I've hit those same walls, and yet – I know beyond the shadow of a doubt I'm walking in my purpose. Over the last 5 years I've published over a dozen books, spoken at churches, universities, and built a vibrant online community for Christians looking to do more with their lives. I've been able to accomplish these things because of the information in this book. This book holds everything I've learned from the Bible about purpose, along with some wisdom from men and women of God who have walked the path of purpose for much longer than I.

This is my gift to you, but more importantly, this is your "permission slip" from God. You don't have to wait until your "good enough." Good enough doesn't exist. All there is, all you can be, is a person dedicated to glorifying God in the profoundly unique way only you can.

When you do that, when you begin to accept where you

are and who you are as enough, that is when amazing things start to happen. And suddenly all those brick walls crumble into stepping stones.

How To Read This Book

This book is a collection of 10 chapters. They all work together and build upon one another, but you don't have to read them in order. If a title or subject captures your eye, feel free to jump ahead!

Think of this work more like a toolbox. Pull out what you need, take the steps you feel God is leading you to take, and then come back and grab another tool when you're ready. This is how I use some of my favorite books, so I wanted to give you the same opportunity.

Ask Me Anything

The best learning happens deeper than level 1. Level 1 is reading a book, listening to a sermon, or memorizing a passage. Level 2, 3, and beyond — these can only be unlocked through asking questions. Lots of questions.

The Bible is busting at the seams with questions. Jesus, the one person in the world who didn't need to ask questions, asked 307 of them during his time on earth. Questions are the core of a growing faith and the foundation of a transforming person.

So ask me! Send me an email here: support@faithspring.org.

Only The Beginning

There's so much more I can say, I want to say, about purpose, calling, the Bible, what Jesus wants for us and what Jesus has for us. But this is the starting point. These few words.

I pray God uses them to do something in your life. We are here only for a few moments, so let's make our moments count.

...I tell you, whoever believes in me will do the works I have been doing, and they will do even greater things than these... John 14:12

Table of Contents

Introduction	iv
6 Fascinating Old Testament Verses That Explain Purpose	1
6 Compelling New Testament Verses That Clarify Purpose	9
5 Types Of Callings You See In The Bible	18
The 1 Question You Must Ask (If You Want To Fulfill Your Calling)	24
What If God Calls Me To Something I Don't Want To Do?	29
How To Make Progress In Your Purpose Even When God Says "No"	38
A Better Definition of Biblical Purpose	47
This Is The Number 1 Purpose Killer (And It's Not Fear…)	55
What's The Difference Between God's Will, God's Plan, and God's Call?	68
Stop Waiting: A Biblical Look At God's Timing	80

Your Next Steps	92
About the Author	94
More Books by David Ramos	95
BONUS: How Trees Survive The Winter (A Guide For Growth In Difficult Times)	97
BONUS: The 10 Best Articles On The Web For Finding Your Purpose	105
BONUS: Every Verse About Purpose In The Bible	115
Endnotes	128

6 Fascinating Old Testament Verses That Explain Purpose

Purpose has been the driving force of God's work in the world since day one.

He made Adam and Eve for a purpose. He called the Israelites to a purpose. And he challenges modern Christians today to join Him in His grand purpose for creation.

You are called to a purpose too. God's children are not just called for the sake of giving them something to keep them busy. Each person is unique. Each human is necessary. And that is why I urge people to take their calling seriously.

Fulfilling your calling is not a selfish endeavor. In fact, pursuing the purpose God has for you is the most *unselfish* thing you can do, because you are surrendering yourself to something infinitely larger than yourself.

You are accepting the invitation God has laid out for you in Scripture and moving God's great plan forward in a way only you can.

But don't just take my word for it. In this article, I will show you 6 of the most powerful verses on purpose in the Old Testament. These will reveal important aspects of God's idea of purpose: how He views purpose, what His expectations are of us, and how we fit into it all.

Exodus 9:16

But I have raised you up for this very purpose, that I might show you my power and that my name might be proclaimed in all the earth.

In the book of Exodus, we find one of the first mentions of the word "purpose" in Scripture. Up to this point in the Biblical narrative, God has been dealing with humans on primarily an individual level. One on one. He walked with Adam, spoke to Abraham, and communicated with Joseph through dreams. But here, God expands and begins to communicate with the nation.

The reason for this expansion is because the purpose He speaks of is too big for any one person or family. It can only be accomplished by a nation, by a people group that will one day be as numerous as the stars themselves. God's purpose for Israel is for God's name to be proclaimed in all the earth. Or put in a different way, God's purpose for us is God's glory.

This calling still sits upon our lives today. Our primary calling in Scripture, as humans, is to glorify God. How that unfolds in our lives through our unique talents, gifts, and circumstances can end up looking a million different ways. But the end goal never changes. We are here for God's glory.

Job 42:2

I know that you can do all things; no purpose of yours can be thwarted.

What would you do if you knew you could not fail? Or better yet, what risk would you take if you knew you were invincible?

It may sound like a silly question, but these questions get to heart of what is being said in Job 42:2. We serve a God who cannot fail. His plans do not go awry. His purposes do not come up empty. When God sets out to accomplish something, it happens – always. He spoke light into existence. He carved us from the dirt. He sacrificed His son for our salvation.

God's plans always go God's way. Now, think about how we fit into this. We are His children, set upon this earth for His reason, and aiming to fulfill His purpose for our lives. If that's true, then why are we so afraid of taking risks? Why are we so disheartened when things seem to be going off-track? God has promised us that His purposes cannot be thwarted.

If we are a part of His purpose – what does that make us? *Unthwartable.*

We might stumble in the short term. But in the grand scheme of things, in the larger picture of what God is doing – there's no way we can fail if we are His.

Psalm 33:11

> *But the plans of the Lord stand firm forever, the purposes of his heart through all generations.*

A puzzle piece doesn't make much sense on its own. It's just a strangely shaped object with some color. If you didn't recognize that it belonged to a puzzle, you would think it was weird, even useless. But, if you were in the process of building a puzzle and you couldn't find that one piece – it would be invaluable to you in that moment! You would turn the house upside down looking for it, because without it, your puzzle would remain unfinished.

You are that puzzle piece to God. You are the unique shape that fits into the grander picture of what He is accomplishing. To people who do not recognize that, who do not understand that you have a role to play, you may appear very strange to them. But to people who are pursuing their own purpose, you will be invaluable, because they will recognize that every person has their part to play. The bigger picture needs all of us.

God's purpose stretches beyond us in ways we could hardly imagine. But it also includes us, intimately.

Proverbs 19:21

Many are the plans in a person's heart, but it is the Lord's purpose that prevails.

Plans are an interesting thing. They're important. You wouldn't trust an architect who told you, "No, I don't really have a plan for how I'm going to build your house but I'll figure it out as I go along." That would be horrible! You wouldn't you trust a doctor who didn't have a plan for your surgery. Even taking it down a level, most of us wouldn't trust a taxi driver who didn't have a plan for getting us to the airport on time!

But plans can only take us so far. You see, plans are preparation. Plans fit onto notecards and into notebooks. They're fun to talk about and brainstorm. But plans only take us up to the starting line, they don't get us running. Purpose does that.

A plan says, here's what I'm going to do and how. If

we're really ambitious, we'll make a Plan B or Plan C just in case things go wrong. But purpose drives us forward regardless of what goes right or wrong. Purpose says, here's the direction I'm going in, and no matter what speedbumps try to stop me, no matter what detours try to derail me, I'm going to keep heading this direction.

When we pray with a plan, we are trying to get God to approve our idea of how things should go. But when we pray with purpose, we are surrendering ourselves to the direction God wants to take us.

Proverbs 20:5

The purpose of a person's heart are deep waters, but one who has insight draws them out.

My wife and I love candles. Every year (especially around winter time) our house is filled with them. One for the bedroom, kitchen, bathroom, and living room. A candle is an amazing little thing, but it's useless without a wick and without a flame.

The candle possesses enough scent to change the mood of an entire room. It already is everything that it needs to be in order to accomplish its unique purpose. But it needs to burn and melt in order for the scent to be released. The fire draws the smell out and enables the candle to fulfill its purpose.

You are the candle. You already are what and who you need to be. It's inside you. God coded it inside of you, down to your very DNA. But in order for that purpose to be released, in order for it to escape and be free to fill up the world it has to be drawn out.

It is God's pleasure to draw out our purpose. He accomplishes this through His Word and His people. Scripture helps us see where God wants to take us, and the people God puts in our lives confirms the direction we are sensing. These are the flames to our candle.

Isaiah 55:11

So is my word that goes out from my mouth: It will not return to me empty, but will accomplish what I desire and achieve the purpose for which I sent it.

This verse in Isaiah comes after a portion of beautiful imagery on rainfall. When the rain comes down upon the earth, it does something. It feeds the plants, it fills the rivers, it washes the world. Every time rain comes, it accomplishes something. The ground is never dissatisfied after a rainfall. It's fed, it's fulfilled. The water comes and the plants grow and the cycle continues because they are fulfilling their purpose.

God's Word is the rainfall to our souls. Every time God's Word comes into contact with a human, something happens. We may not see it. It may not grow anything that day, that year, or that decade. But it starts something, because God promises that His Word will never return to Him empty.

Just as God's Word accomplishes God's purpose, the Bible also enables us to accomplish great things. When we are watered by God's truths, we can't help but grow into pillars of God's work in the world. That's how God shaped it to be. It's almost as formulaic as a math problem. 2 + 2 has to equal 4, because it does. God's Word has to accomplish something, it has to shape us, it has to grow us into the people of purpose He desires us to be, because that was His purpose for it. And we benefit because of it.

Thank you for reading this and discovering just a taste of what the Old Testament has to say about purpose. I hope you will take these to heart. Continue to seek out God's wisdom for your direction, and remember that pursuing your calling is one of the least selfish and most God-glorifying actions you can take!

6 Compelling New Testament Verses That Clarify Purpose

Jesus was the perfect human. He was an example of what God intended His creation to be. Jesus' relationship with God was a model for what ours could be, and will be, as we grow towards Him. Jesus' life was also a model of purpose.

Everything in Scripture was leading towards a climax: the coming, the death, and the resurrection of Jesus Christ. God had a reason for Jesus being here. Jesus had a profound purpose that will ripple across time itself and impact every human being.

So if Jesus was the example, the pinnacle, of what a human ought to be – then how is it possible for any of us to deny that we too were created for a purpose. Just as God sent Jesus to earth for a reason, He sent us for a reason as well. When God made you, He had something in mind for you to do. He knew that by putting you into this world, at this moment in history, with this group of people, you could bring Him glory in a profoundly beautiful and unique way.

Just as Scripture built towards Jesus' purpose, it also has so much to tell us about our own. In this chapter, you'll discover 6 Bible verses from the New Testament that will illuminate your purpose and encourage your heart to step into the life God has always planned for you.

Acts 5:38

Therefore, in the present case I advise you: Leave these men alone! Let them go! For if their purpose or activity is of human origin, it will fail.

This scene appears in the middle of a heated conflict between the apostles and the Sanhedrin (a particular group of Pharisees). The apostles had been fulfilling their mission and suffering greatly for it. They kept pushing, despite their difficulties, because God was leading them forward. One of the Sanhedrin leaders sees this and, before the apostles could be kicked out of the city, stands before his Pharisee peers to plead their case.

He says, in essence – look, we keep fighting against this message, but maybe they are correct. If we were just fighting against men we would have won already, but if we are fighting against God we will never win!

God is responsible for fulfilling the purpose He has for our lives. Read that last sentence again!

Do you see how freeing this is? If we were responsible for finding our purpose and then making it happen, we would fail. But God didn't design it that way. He's promised us that since He is the one who sent us, He would be the one to make sure we are successful.

When you surrender yourself to fulfilling God's purpose for your life, you can have all the confidence in the universe that you will succeed, because the One who holds the universe is on your side.

Romans 8:28

And we know that in all things God works for the good of those who love him, who have been called according to his purpose.

On the internet, there is a device called "social proof." Social proof is the technique where creators and salespeople use the positive words other people have said to convince you that you can trust them (with your business, money, time, etc.). They do this by showing how many social media followers they have, or how many testimonials they've gotten. They want you to identify with the others and say, if that person trusted you, then I can too.

God has the strangest *and* the most powerful social proof in existence. On the one hand, he has stories of his closet, most devoted followers suffering greatly because they have surrendered their lives to His will. Yet at the same time, all of creation from the birds of the air to the trees themselves praise God for His goodness and wisdom. God has all the universe vouching that you can trust Him, and yet we struggle.

If we really believed this verse, our lives would be so much simpler, and so much more effective. God's purpose in our lives is always for our good. Nature knows this, the angels believe this, the apostles can see this. We must put on this belief as well.

Romans 9:20-21

But who are you, a human being, to talk back to God? Shall what is formed say to the one who formed it, Why did you make me like this? Does not the potter have the right to make out of the same lump of clay some pottery for special purposes and some for common use?

This verse is a hard one. If this was a thanksgiving dinner, this would be the one you'd be asked to put away because it isn't "polite conversation."

God, as the potter, has complete control and dominion over what he can create, and over what he can task that creation with doing. It's his pleasure to decide. It's his right, as ruler, to assign: some for special purposes and some for common use.

If you're reading this, I wholeheartedly believe you are one of the few set aside for a "special purpose." How do I know that? Because the ones who were destined for common use never bother desiring more. They settle. They sit on the shelves in their beige color and perform whatever task has been assigned to them. They're consistent and we need them. But don't for one minute think that you are useless because you aren't shaped like they are.

A planting pot can be very large. It can hold a huge plant along with gallons of water. Another vessel may be used for holding drinking water. This one is smaller, but what it holds is vital to life. And finally, the smallest container could be one for medicine. It may look minuscule beside the other vessels, but what it holds is transformative and valuable.

God does not want us to compare our purpose to one another because everyone is necessary. But don't ever forget, the strangest vessels usually have the most important purposes.

1 Corinthians 3:8

The one who plants and the one who waters have one purpose, and they will each be rewarded according to their own labor.

Farming is a long and tedious process. A large field of land requires numerous hands to work it. And each worker has a unique task. Some use machines to till the soil. Others are experts at laying the seeds. There are a few who must water and fertilize. Down the line, some may need to weed or prune the plants. And on and on it goes until finally, after dozens of workers have touched the plant with their specialty, is someone able to harvest it.

Like the example above, we are all working together for God's grand purpose. Our purposes build upon one another. I am a teacher of God's Word, but in the grand scheme of things I am only a small part of the larger process. Before you came to this chapter on purpose, there had to be dozens of people and encounters before me who helped you come to a place where you could know Jesus and recognize that maybe your life truly did have a unique calling. I am here to serve my part, and afterward, you will move on and another part of God's family will serve theirs.

Remember this as you try to figure out where you fit into God's grand scheme of things. Our calling will require other believers. As we step closer to our purpose, we will need the body, the church, more and more. God designed it that way for our good.

Ephesians 3:11

According to his eternal purpose that he accomplished in Christ Jesus our Lord.

Whenever I complete a video game I love, I always go back and start over from the beginning. The second time through, the game is a completely different experience. I notice things I didn't notice before. I take different risks; I choose different options; my whole attitude about it has changed. I'm a different player the second time through because I've already won.

When you know how it ends, you play with a confidence that is hard to describe. It's like you're safe no matter what happens because you know you will win, so you allow yourself to take risks you otherwise wouldn't have the first time around.

This is the kind of life God wants us to live. He wants us to live from the knowledge that we have already won! God's ultimate purpose has already been accomplished. Jesus "sealed the deal" if you will. He was both the finale and the introduction. He is the lamb who was slain and the king who has conquered. And we are His.

When we live, we do so out of victory. Out of the abundance of God's success, not from the desperation of not knowing. We play from our winnings and that changes everything.

Hebrews 6:17

Because God wanted to make the unchanging nature of his purpose very clear to the heirs of what was promised, he confirmed it in an oath.

When this verse talks about the "unchanging nature" of God's purpose, what it's really talking about is the word consistency.

Consistency is the attribute of "not varying...over time."[i] Things that are consistent "hold together." They keep going. They show up on time and always perform as promised. I believe one of the reasons consistency is such a common trait among the world's most successful people is because it reflects one of the most core attributes of God.

God is, by His nature, the very definition of consistency. And when He spoke His purpose to Abraham, when He first invited humans into His grand remaking of creation, God was not telling us about a weekend project He was taking on. He was allowing us to see a glimpse of His consistent nature.

God's purpose and character is unchanging. The reason that matters for us is because it lays a foundation stronger than bedrock for us to stand on. We, as humans, change often and a lot. We are by our very nature inconsistent. The fact that God would choose us to be His image-bearers is in itself a violent paradox. But it doesn't have to stay that way.

God's consistency invites us to be consistent as well. To take hold of our purpose and to never let go. To not be swayed or distracted. To put on blinders and march, step by step, towards the destination God has placed upon our hearts.

God's consistency should not be alarming, but comforting. It means He won't change His mind about us. No matter the failure. No matter the struggle. He'll be there.

Thank you for reading these 6 powerful verses on purpose. I hope they will drive you to read God's Word more, and believe that while you still have breath in your body, God has something for you to accomplish. We serve a great God of purpose and His invitation to you is loud and clear.

5 Types Of Callings You See In The Bible

What's my calling?

I've heard this question asked a million times during my years in ministry. I've probably asked the question a million times myself.

Once you get into the subject of calling and purpose, you can't get very far before the question begins to change. We realize that this whole idea of calling isn't as simple as we once made it out to be, and if we are going to successfully identify our calling, then there's another question we have to answer first:

What does a calling look like?

In this chapter5 you will discover the five main frameworks of how callings enter our lives, along with Biblical examples of each one. My hope is that you'll take some time and self-evaluate which calling God may be using in your life right now (or which one might be right around the corner). Being able to identify a calling is one of the first steps towards fulfilling it.

1. Situational

Here's a question for you: was Ruth called to serve Naomi? I believe she was.

She left everything behind for this elderly woman, not knowing how any of it would turn out. The heavens didn't open up or an angel descend and tell her that this was something she needed to do. Rather, she simply observed her options and took the opportunity that was in front of her to love another person.

Sometimes our callings are that simple. Rather than inviting us to some grand adventure, God first asks us to observe, to pay attention, and to love. Maybe the person or situation we believe is a roadblock to our call is actually the call itself.

2. Disruption

Multiple times throughout the Biblical narrative we see normal people have their lives turned upside down and set upon an entirely new course by a divine disruption.

In Genesis 12, we see God call Abraham and tell him to

move to a new land. In Luke 1, we see an angel tell the virgin Mary she's pregnant with God's son!

These are not the typical sort of calls we see in our lives, or in Scripture, but they do occur. So how do we prepare for a disruption? We don't (hence the name!). But what we can do is learn to recognize God's voice, so that we might answer when He calls.

3. Pain-Driven

In the book of Nehemiah, we see a man who is driven to repair the destruction of Jerusalem. He sees the pain in his people's eyes and it moves him to action.

All of us will experience pain in this life. For some, that pain will move us into action as well. When pain becomes a negative motivator, it looks like revenge and self-destruction. But pain can also be a positive motivator. When it is driven by that positive light, its ultimate goal is to seek and share healing.

Nehemiah helped heal God's people by addressing their pain. What might your pain be calling you to heal?

4. Missional

The disciple Peter experienced nearly every type of call in his life. Jesus disrupted his life, brought him into painful and trying situations, and finally crowned him with a commission that would revolutionize the world (Matthew 28).

The final, and possibly most powerful, call on Peter's life (along with the disciples) was the mission of spreading God's truth and love to all nations. Jesus left them a job to do, and that assignment became their purpose, their drive, and their calling.

We each have our role to play in the Great Commission. Usually, our mission is much more specific. Through some event, or word, or relationship, we are given the mission to reach a certain people group or create a certain product – and we drive our lives towards that goal (regardless of how clear or unclear it may be).

5. Passion-Driven

To be passionate means to love something so much, you are willing to suffer for it. Jesus was the pinnacle of the passion-driven calling. It was because "God so loved the world" that Jesus came in the first place. And it was his passion that carried him to the hungry, to the forgotten, and ultimately to the cross.

This is a rare call, and it's even rarer to see people follow it. A life driven by passion is a life surrendered. Everything you are becomes about that thing you love, and the hope that others might love it as well.

These are the five types of callings you will see across Scripture. There may be more types, and many times, these can blend together. But what I want you to remember is this truth: you are called. There is something, some purpose, uniquely designed for you. And how you get introduced to it will likely come from one of these five ways.

Quick Recap of 5 Types:

Situational – Observe your life and take the next clear step (it will usually require love and some sacrifice).

Disruption – Through some divine (or other) interruption, your life is dramatically altered and you are clearly set upon a different path.

Pain-Driven – Seek to share healing with others because of observing their pain or acknowledging your own.

Missional – Pulled towards something bigger than yourself that was confirmed through various elements in your life.

Passion-Driven – Surrendered, out of love, to some costly goal or idea.

Additional Biblical Examples:

Situational – Jacob (leaves family), Esther (risks queenship), Daniel (resisting the evil laws)

Disruption – Samuel (called as child), David (chosen as king), Amos (farmer turned prophet)

Pain-Driven – Absalom (avenges sister), Joseph (forgives brothers), Job (seeks truth about God)

Missional – Jonah (goes to Nineveh), Moses (free Israelites), Paul (bring Gospel to Gentiles)

Passion-Driven – Enoch (taken to God), Hosea (loves people and family), John the Baptist (love for the Savior)

The 1 Question You Must Ask (If You Want To Fulfill Your Calling)

Before I began writing my first book, I remember feeling one emotion more than any other: *overwhelm*.

I was overwhelmed by the scope of what I wanted to accomplish. Overwhelmed by the calling I felt God leading me towards. Overwhelmed by the amount of work I would have to do. And, quite honestly, terrified that I was nowhere near ready to travel this path.

I am a natural planner, so my mind immediately jumped to steps 5, 10, and 50. I wanted to know the entire journey before I ever took the first step. But that desire was just a defense mechanism for the fear I felt.

Fear that I wasn't enough. Fear that what I made wouldn't be good enough. And fear that I would fail the call God had given me.

That is, until I learned how to transform my mindset by

asking a single question. This question rescued me from my fear and put the emotion of overwhelm in check. It's also the same question we see some of the greatest heroes of Scripture ask during their pivotal moments.

Abraham is one of my favorite characters in the Bible. His story is foundational to the Biblical narrative. Without him we would miss out on so many promises, so many beautiful pictures of God's character, and ultimately, there would be no Israel.

So how did this great character answer Gods call? If you remember, Abraham's (Abram's) call was unique because it was so unclear.

Go from your country, your people and your father's household to the land I will show you.
Genesis 12:1

God asked Abraham to simply go. No destination, no big end goal, no clear sign. Just a promise and a direction. It was in that uncertainty and confusion that Abraham had to make a choice. He could either be overwhelmed (like I was and like so many Christians are) or he could ask himself the one question:

What is the next right step?

You see, for Abraham to be faithful he didn't have to know all of the answers. He didn't have to understand or agree with God's grand plan. All he had to do was move one step in the right direction. That's it.

That was the key for me as well. As soon as I stopped trying to map out where God's journey would take me and how I would get there, I was free to just be in the moment. Free to be at peace in the uncertainty, to feel as though I didn't need to be "enough" all at once, right now. All I needed to do was identify the next right step, and God would take care of the rest.

So often we disable our ability to answer our call by trying to shrink it into our ideas of how these things ought to work. But God knows what He is doing. I guarantee you, one of the purposes of His call on your life is to develop greater trust in Him. We see this truth over and over again in Scripture. People are taken on unbelievable adventures and pushed to trust God like never before.

Your word is a lamp for my feet, a light on my path.
Psalm 119:105

I want you to imagine this. It's pitch black outside and all you have is a small candle-lit lamp that you are holding out in front of you. How far ahead of you does this lamp light up? Maybe a few feet at most. I believe the writer of this psalm chose this image on purpose. God's Word is a lamp, not a street light. It only helps us see what is next. Not steps 5, 10, or 50 down the road.

Therefore do not worry about tomorrow, for tomorrow will worry about itself. Each day has enough trouble of its own. Matthew 6:34

Over and over again God is trying to get us to expand our trust by limiting our view. We don't need trust if we know every obstacle and triumph that will come our way. But we do need trust if all we can see, if all we can think about and focus on is our today, our now, and our next right step.

What The Next Right Step Gets Us

Clarity

You can have clarity even in the midst of uncertainty. I know it sounds contradictory, but think about it. If you are driving through a thick fog, you may not know what is 2 miles in front of you. But you can see the small stretch of road that is directly in front of you. You don't know a lot, but you know enough. And that small amount enables you to have confidence that the next step is the right one.

Action

What's your reaction to being overwhelmed? I know

what mine is: freeze up or give up. When I'm overwhelmed my whole body and mind begin to shut down. It's like a highway during rush hour traffic. When too many cars are all trying to get somewhere at the same time, traffic screeches to crawl (or even a complete stop).

But when you ask yourself "what is the next right step" it cancels the feeling of overwhelm. It's like opening up a detour on the overcrowded highway – you don't need to fit every car through the detour, just yours. And it might not get you to your destination, but it's going to get you moving in the right direction. Asking this simple question will get you moving as well.

Obedience

A calling is not a commandment, but there is an element of obedience present in fulfilling your purpose. When you ask what's the next right step, you are humbling yourself before God. You are admitting your need for guidance on this journey, as well as revealing your desire to serve God in the unique way He has asked you. This is a submission to God's authority, and an act of obedience. I believe the Bible shows that obedience begets clarity, and when clarity is present, action is inevitable. And once we have taken action, the journey towards our calling has truly begun.

So then, what is your next right step?

What If God Calls Me To Something I Don't Want To Do?

What if God calls me to something I hate?
To a place I never wanted to go?
To people I can't stand being around?
To a job that brings me no joy?

This question is a very real concern for many Christians. Growing up, I learned that God will likely call us to painful, life-long missions of service. That if we want to be obedient children of God, we need to learn how to say yes. No argument. No complaining. Because faithful servants don't gripe. They answer their call, suffering as needed, and then get rewarded in Heaven.

Something in that message didn't sit right with me. I hadn't yet explored the Bible in great depths, so I didn't have any ammunition to fight what they were saying. But still, an invisible rock would form in my stomach every time I heard them teach about calling and purpose.

When I was older, I was exposed to a very different point of view. These new teachers explained how God does not want us to live painful lives. After all, how do poor, beaten down people bring glory to God? What God wants is successful people. Followers who are following their dreams and accomplishing great things for God's kingdom.

Again, something didn't sit right with me. Their message, while enticing, seemed incomplete. I didn't know in what way, but I knew that I had to go to Scripture to find out.

So I did, and I want to share with you what I discovered.

Below are 3 lies, or false assumptions, we make about our callings, followed by 3 truths. After we tackle those six, I'll give you my answer to the question: Would God call us to something we do not enjoy?

3 Lies You Believe About Your Calling

1. God must call me to something difficult and painful for it to be worthwhile.

Somewhere along the way, our Christian culture has picked up the idea that the more a servant suffers, the better or higher their calling is.

I can understand why some believe this. The New Testament is filled with servants of God suffering greatly (John the Baptist, Paul, Jesus). However, those were individuals with a very unique calling located in a very unique time in history.

If you look back to the Old Testament, we can see Jabez stepping into his calling – not through pain and death, but through prayer and provision. In the New Testament, Luke fulfills his calling as a writer and goes on to live well into old age. As church history stretched on, the vast majority of Christians came into their callings by way of perseverance and joy, not persecution and tears.

You will face pain in this life. You may even face additional challenges on your way towards purpose. But don't for a second believe that what God has for you is a misery-ridden task.

2. *God is more concerned about the work that has to be done than our joy.*

"...for God loves a cheerful giver." 2 Corinthians 9:7b

"A person can do nothing better than to eat and drink and find satisfaction in their work." Ecclesiastes 2:24

John Piper was one of the main Bible teachers to shape me while I was in college. These days, we disagree on a number of topics. But I think his idea of Christian Hedonism was absolutely a gift.

Christian Hedonism says this, "God is most glorified in us when we are most satisfied in Him." In this phrasing, our joy becomes an avenue for God's glory.

Think about that. If God's reason for creation is His glory, and His glory is directly tied to our joy, then how important do you think our joy is to God? Extremely important!

Throughout the Bible we see examples of God brushing aside gifts and sacrifices because they were performed out of duty, not from a place of joy. Whether God wants the work accomplished or our joy fulfilled is not an either/or. It's an *and*. God wants both: the work of restoration complete *and* the joy of His people fulfilled.

His glory requires both.

> 3. *We must be highly skilled in something in order to be called to it.*

In Exodus 31, God speaks to Moses about who He has chosen to build His tabernacle. Bezalel, Aholiab, and many other "gifted artisans" are given the task of building a truly magnificent place for God's spirit to reside. This is a rare Biblical example of God calling uniquely qualified individuals to complete a skill-intensive task.

Besides this example, it would be faster to list everyone who was qualified in Scripture than it would be to list all of the under- (or just completely un-) qualified people God called.

You've probably heard the phrase "God does not call the qualified, He qualifies the called." It may be cliché, but there's a ton of truth in that statement.

The pattern of God's calling throughout Scripture is that He summons humans who need to rely on Him in order to accomplish what He has set out for them to do. Because of this pattern, the vast majority of the called are not highly skilled. But through the events God orchestrates, they develop the exact skills they need.

3 Truths About Your Calling

1. Our purpose will require more than we are capable of.

"But he said to me, "My grace is sufficient for you, for my power is made perfect in weakness." 2 Corinthians 12:9

Your calling will ask more of you than you are able to give, and this is a good thing.

Esther is an excellent example of this. She was a fierce woman of God, with immense wit and character. Yet even she needed the help of others around her in order for her to accomplish the goal of saving the Jewish people. Mordecai, the king, and so many others played a vital role in her story. Not to mention God's continual, unseen hand.

Your calling will necessitate you to join, or build, a community. That is the pattern we see throughout Scripture. Jesus – the literal Savior – did not begin by building a church, or starting a street ministry. Instead, one of his first major actions was to recruit a community of 12 followers, the disciples.

In the same way, as we move deeper into what we are here to do, it should become more apparent that we can never accomplish our calling alone.

2. *Both the worker and the work have a unique shape.*

"And it was He who gave some to be apostles, some to be prophets, some to be evangelists, and some to be pastors and teachers" Ephesians 4:11

Do you believe you are unique? It's a question I want you to answer honestly.

I ask this because what people say and what they do often contradict. They'll say, "yes, God made me unique" – and then they'll spend their entire lives trying to copy other people, pursuing goals that were never meant for them to accomplish.

By being a unique creation of God, you were given a

shape. A shape that no one else can replace. Now, there may be similarities between your shape and the shape of others, but there are also important differences. And those differences matter if you are going to find and do the "work" that was uniquely shaped for you.

We constantly use the analogy of trying to fit a round peg into a square hole, but we keep trying anyway! There are an infinite number of ways to bring God glory, and I guarantee the one God has for you will fit like the glass slipper did on Cinderella.

3. You will find joy and excellence in your calling.

"The secret of joy in work is contained in one word – excellence. To know how to do something well is to enjoy it." – Pearl S. Buck

One of the essential qualities of finding work you love is the ability to become better at it.

What you'll often find at the highest level of performers is that they didn't start off loving every aspect of their profession. But they had a spark of passion, and a commitment to hard work. Over time, that hard work led them to develop skills, and those skills transformed into excellence.

And now, their excellence is what produces joy.

The same structure applies to the work God has for you.

Moses was a not a natural leader. But by the end of Deuteronomy, we see a completely different person. A pillar of faith who has become an excellent example of a life devoted to God. Even though he was unable to enter the Promised Land with his people, he found joy in the journey and satisfaction in taking them so far.

"The Rock, his work is perfect, for all his ways are justice." Deuteronomy 32:4

Your calling may be sparked by passion, but it will be set aflame by excellence. Devote yourself to becoming great at the purpose God has for you, and He will use it in ways you couldn't even imagine.

So, would God call us to something we do not enjoy? *It's the wrong question.*

Will God call us to difficult things? *Yes.*

Will our calling be painful at times? *Absolutely.*

Will God enable us to enjoy the work and process of our purpose? *Without a doubt.*

Your calling, the macro-reason you are here, will always outshine the micro-pains which will try to stop you. That does not mean those pains will be small; nor does it mean that there won't be major delays and detours.

I just believe we need to take Philippians 1:6 more seriously, "He who began a good work in you will carry it on to completion until the day of Christ Jesus." Our calling is ultimately God's duty to fulfill. We are messengers, vessels, pots of clay carrying a glory we could hardly describe.

The work is our gift, but we never labor alone.

How To Make Progress In Your Purpose Even When God Says "No"

It wasn't something I necessarily wanted. But the opportunity had come to me. They called me. The door had opened precisely when I was looking at other doors to walk through. But just as quickly as it appeared, it vanished. The opportunity pulled away and I was left confused and disappointed. I had gotten my hopes up. I believed this was the path God had for me. But I was wrong, and it hurt.

Then, just like that, a different path opened…but we'll get to that.

There have been three times in my life when I have pursued an opportunity that seemingly fit my calling, only to have it shut down right before my eyes. I'm going to tell you about those three events now. To some of you, they won't sound very devastating. Some of us are built to withstand rejection better than others. Some, like me, crumble before it. I'm working on it, but rejection has a way of attacking my self-worth in a way nothing else can.

The positive part of this story, the redeeming part, is that I did find a path. And how I got there matters ... a lot.

Rejection #1

I was young and ambitious. Naïve – yes. But I more than made up for that in hard work and perseverance. I completed my undergraduate studies, had a few years of ministry experience under my belt, and was a candidate for a full-time position in a non-profit that helped inner city youth. It would have been an opportunity to live out the Gospel I dedicated so much time to studying. I would have the opportunity to teach small Bible studies, mentor youth, support an organization I believed in, and get paid while doing so.

It seemed like a match made in Heaven. Like something God wanted me to do.

It's interesting how when things start to line up in our minds, one of our first thoughts (as Christians) is that God must want me to do this. We read the stories about David finding smooth stones or Rebekah's discovery by Abraham's servant and assume that our callings will line up in a similar way.

The organization liked me and I liked them. I got the call back with an opportunity to shadow for a full day and meet some key people. Everything appeared as though it was headed in the right direction. I was perfect for what they needed; and they were perfect for me.

Until I got the last phone call. The phone call that told me they had gone with someone else. The phone call where I'll never remember what they actually said. All I remember hearing is God telling me *no*.

Rejection #2

Disheartened but no less determined, I enrolled in seminary.

My time in seminary was, by far, some of the most difficult years of my life. The actual seminary work: reading, writing, preaching, designing – that was fine. I loved that part.

What you learn, if you ever attend seminary, is that God uses that time to accomplish something inside of you that cannot be accomplished any other way except through pain. I witnessed this in so many of my classmates. Everyone's pain looks different. But it's always exactly the sort of pain you need to develop strength where you need it most.

It was also during this time that I felt my calling shift. If the door to me being a youth worker was closed, then the next thing my heart wanted most was to become a professor.

Again, like so many things, it made sense! I excelled in my classes. I gained the opportunity to travel with my professors, to sit in on presentations, and to debate complicated research topics that would guide my studies.

I felt like I fit in. They could have been my people. This could have been my path.

I met with my advisor to talk through how I felt I was being led and, to my surprise, I received an answer I was not expecting.

Like the phone call, I can't tell you what he said. But I can remember what I felt. I felt sick. I felt like running away. I felt like dropping out right then and there because again...God was telling me *no*.

Rejection #3

I graduated seminary and began working at a local college. I wasn't teaching, but my position enabled me to mentor others, to help students, and to grow as a leader. I grew quickly there. But still, it didn't feel like this was it – like this was the place to invest my whole self. It was a necessary step, but only just that – a step on the journey towards something (and somewhere) else.

In my own time, I began writing and teaching about the Bible. My efforts gained an audience, and before long another opportunity came knocking. This one was close to home: I was asked to consider becoming a pastor. A real pastor, with souls to shepherd and lives to grow. A responsibility I wasn't sure I could handle, but then again, taking on more than we can handle is how we grow into being able to handle more.

I don't have to tell you what happened, you know where this is going. The opportunity to become a pastor, one that took over my prayers and thought life for months on end, quickly revealed that it would have been like trying to fit a square peg into a round whole. I wasn't the right fit. God had seemingly opened another door only to tell me *no* once more.

There are a few things I learned about when God says no, and I want to share those with you in the hope that you'll be both comforted and encouraged. The path towards purpose is a twisty one. It's filled with detours and U-turns, but I promise if you listen to God's no's as much as His yeses you'll get to exactly the place you need to be.

God's no will save you pain.

When I look back at the rejections I received, I can see that each one saved me from a pain I couldn't see at the moment. The pain may have been financial trouble, relational turmoil, or unnecessary emotional risk. I couldn't understand it in the moment, but afterward, down the road and past the short-term pain of hearing another *no* I could see the benefit and thank God for His abundant wisdom.

God's no is always, always, always for your good.

God's no will save you time.

Most people think that I am a patient person. If you ask my wife, you'll discover the opposite is true. I just hide it better than most!

In geometry we learn that the shortest distance between any two points is a straight line. In our journeys, those two points are where we are now (frustrated, hustling, not using our gifts) and where we want to be (fulfilling our calling, joyful, useful). Life is not geometry. The shortest distance between where you are and where you want to be is never going to be a straight line.

In life, the shortest distance between here and there is through God's no's.

You see, those of us who hear God say no are brave enough to do something in the first place! The ones who always hear yes are either asking too small, or too rarely. It's the ones who hear no, the ones who need to be redirected and rerouted that end up accomplishing great things for God.

Abraham, Moses, Esther, David, Joseph, Jesus – all of these heroes heard no on their journeys. So take heart; if you've been told no by God you're closer to your calling than you think.

God's no will save you from yourself.

I would have made a great youth worker, professor, or pastor. But if any of those had been yeses I would likely have never met my wife. I would have never wrote my first book – which led to a dozen more being written after it. I would have never met some of the most important people who are in my life today. I would certainly not be writing this, to you, now.

When I read John 10:10b, I don't see it is a far-off promise that applies to a heavenly existence. I see it as something that has real meaning and weight for this life on earth. Right here. Right now.

> *I have come that [you] may have life,*
> *and have it to the full.*

God's no will prevent you from becoming the you you think you could be, so that you can become the you God's knows you can be.

God made you, and because of that, I guarantee His perceptions of your potential are infinitely higher than your own. Don't settle.

The 1 Thing To Do

So what's the answer for finding the right path? How do we finally get God's yes? I believe, wholeheartedly, that the answer begins with a yes from and to ourselves.

Yes – I am worthy of God's love and plan for my life because of Jesus.

Yes – I am here for a purpose and my time spent on this earth, however long or short, will be effective.

Yes – I believe I have a gift the world needs. My job is to be faithful in it, and God will take care of the results.

Remember, that every time God says no He is only saying it to the opportunity, not to you. When He looks at you, His answer is always yes.

Yes – you are mine.

Yes – you are here for a reason.

Yes – my plans for you are good.

David Ramos

A Better Definition of Biblical Purpose

One of the most useful traits I've picked up during my life is a love for language. When you study words, you discover truths that most people never get. There's a mystery and a beauty to the language we speak. We can say one thing, but mean another. We can develop code words, or learn new languages. Language is a universal tool that every human uses, and yet it remains deeply intimate. The words we use define us. And the way we understand those words defines us as well – whether those definitions are accurate or not.

In my work on the subjects of calling and purpose I've run into all sorts of definitions for those words. Some useful, others not so much. In this chapter, I want to give you the most accurate Biblical definition of what purpose means. I believe once you discover God's intent for purpose, you'll never pursue it the same way again.

Standard Definitions

If you do a quick search for the definition of the word purpose, you'll get some of the following answers:[ii]

The reason for which something exists

Determination; resoluteness

A goal to be accomplished or an object to be reached

All of these should sound familiar to us. They're also not wrong. When we think about purpose, we are trying to get to the "reason" behind something. Our *why*. Just like we can identify the reason, or usefulness, of a toaster or a screwdriver – we often think our purpose can be that straightforward as well.

It's also true that purpose can be a driving force behind our efforts. When we let our purpose motivate us we're able to work harder, longer, and accomplish much more than those who are motivated by their basic needs, or, like so many people, by fear.

Finally, we often set up purpose to be something outside of ourselves. Our purpose may be to accomplish *X* or become the first *blank*. Those are all well and good, but they can also become disheartening because we can strive our entire lives only to never fulfill our purpose if the thing we want eludes us.

I believe Scripture has a better definition for us. One that empowers us, gives direction to our action, and ties our calling into the heart of God.

What The Bible Says About Purpose

In a previous chapter we tackled the various references there are to purpose in the bible. Since translators have some freedom when they are bringing words over from Greek and Hebrew into English, we found anywhere from 34 – 77 "purpose" references in the Bible (most translations have somewhere around 50).

Because of that wide range, I knew that relying on the English words alone would not accomplish everything we needed, so I decided to pull out the language materials and do some digging into what the original languages had to say about purpose.

Just as a disclaimer, I am not a language expert. I did take both Greek and Hebrew in seminary (although I failed Hebrew the first time around…nobody's perfect!), and I continue to brush up on my language skills regularly. I believe in the value of what I am going to write below, and I sincerely hope you find it valuable as well.

Purpose in Ancient Greek

Through my research I discovered at least 8 words in New Testament Greek which can be translated into purpose:[iii]

Βούλημα, γνώμη, νόημα, μετανοέω, δωρεάν, ἱνατί, προτίθεμαι, πρόθεσις

(boulema, gnome, noema, metanoeo, dorean, hinati, protithemi, prothesis)

Each of these words have different nuances about them. *Boulema* and *gnome* have more to do with decision making and using one's knowledge to determine a direction. *Noema* and *metanoeo* deal with a person's mind, and how their thoughts influence their action.

Dorean is actually more specifically about a free gift. But it speaks about a gift that lacks a purpose, meaning that no repayment is required or that there is no expectation given with the gift, which I thought gave an interesting color to the word purpose and how it comes paired with certain "expectations."

Finally, *protithemi* and *prothesis* are both concerned with the before. A purpose must be planned and strategized before it is pursued or executed.

As you can see, purpose has a broad history. The words which give us our word for purpose have their own agendas and deeper meanings. It's impossible to catch everything they are trying to convey in a single English word. However, before we move on to the Hebrew I do want to pull out a few major themes:

- The mind or thoughts, are an essential part of one's purpose
- Purpose exists before it is recognized
- There is an expectation around purpose. Not so much a demand, but more like an invitation to be fulfilled

Purpose in Ancient Hebrew

In my study of Hebrew, I came across 10 words which could be translated into purpose but only 9 of which fit what we are trying to do here:[iv]

שָׁלָל, מַחֲשָׁבָה, עֵצָה, רֵעַ, הַצְּדָא, מְזִמָּה, יֵצֶר, מַעַן, זָמַם

(shalal, machashabah, etsah, rea, tseda, mezimmah, yetser, maan, zamam)

Side Note: The English transliterations are written left to right to correspond with their Hebrew words in a left to right order, even though Hebrew is read right to left.

What I first noticed when going through the Hebrew definitions is that there was a lot more cohesion across different words. Nearly all of them had something to do with our or God's mind and thought life (*mezimmah, zamam, yetser, etsah, machashabah, rea*). These words dealt with the ideas of imagination, advice, considering the outcomes, and curiosity.

In the Old Testament, so much of what we think of as purpose took place in and stemmed from the Israelites thought-life. They saw the two as intimately connected, and we'll talk about this some more below.

There were also a few interesting words like *tseda* which carried the idea of truth, and *shalal* which means to pull or draw out (like a grain from a sack, but also like plundering and taking what is not yours).

Although more targeted, the Hebrew, as with the Greek, presents a wide range of possible meanings for the word purpose. Here's what I found to be most helpful and important to take away:

- A person's thought and a person's purpose were essentially the same thing in Hebrew
- Purpose is a neutral word and can be guided towards negative or positive directions
- Purpose is the start of something, it leads to action

A Better Definition of Purpose

As I studied through my notes and tried to make sense of all the information I was seeing, a better definition started to rise to the surface.

If you think through what we covered above, purpose is intimately linked to the mind. But it also requires action, commitment, and direction. Purpose is not something we create. Rather, we pick it up; we step into or uncover it. And, Biblically speaking, purpose is something God is always at the center of. Either we are chasing, fulfilling, being guided by His purpose – or we are avoiding it, dodging it, and usurping it with our own desire.

So here's my definition of purpose, built off the original words and what they were trying to convey:

Purpose is to listen to, and then step in line with, the thoughts of God.

God's thoughts are before us (*protithemi, prosthesis*) and His thoughts are truth (*tseda*). All of the words dealing with thought, decision making, and the mind find their home in this definition. God's mind, His thoughts, are the origin of purpose and are what set us towards meaningful action.

I think one of the most powerful aspects of this definition is that it exists completely outside of ourselves. Purpose is not something that originates inside of us. It is not something we create. Instead, it is something God has and that we are invited into.

When we are trying to find our calling, or our purpose, what we are really trying to do is uncover God's original thoughts about us. What did He have in mind when He created us? For what reason are we here? What path does He have for us to walk?

We can exist without living our purpose. We can even live a good life without it. But we cannot live a truly full life without it. We cannot fully please God if we spend our time on this earth ignoring His thoughts about us.

I pray you found this definition of Biblical purpose helpful and that you will take your calling seriously. God has thoughts about you – beautiful thoughts. Part of your calling is to find out what those are.

This Is The Number 1 Purpose Killer (And It's Not Fear...)

In my third year of college, I had the opportunity to help lead and organize a game for an event called Junior Jam. To help you understand the scale of this event: approximately 800-1000 kids (ages 8-12) would all descend upon the college campus for a 12-hour day full of activities. Hundreds of churches, leaders, and students would organize the day. There would be food, speakers, a concert, and the main attraction: 4-6 "games" that tied in with that year's theme.

These games were somewhat legendary. I had a partner, who was also a college junior, a dozen student helpers, and roughly $1,000 to entertain 200 kids at a time for 45 minutes. All to make something these kids would rave about when they went back home to their families.

That year's theme was purity, but in a G-rated way. Our theme song was "Be careful little eyes what you see."

Each game station took a particular body part and formed an activity around it. There was the eyes, the hands (be careful what you do), the feet (be careful where you go), and the ears (be careful what you hear). We had the ears.

Our game was simple, but (in my opinion) kind of brilliant. Let me explain how it worked.

The large group of 200 kids was divided into their section leaders (usually 1-2 per 8-10 kids). These kids would have already spent a few hours with their leader. They would have gotten to know them and, hopefully, recognize their voice. We separated the students from the leaders by lining up the students along the floor lines in the gym and placing the leaders about 30-40 feet away in colored circles. Two-hundred kids on one side, 20 leaders on the other.

Before we separated them, we gave each leader a recognizable sound (a roar, a horn, a word, etc.) and had them share it with their group. The task of the game was for the students to listen for their leader's sound and make their way over to them. The brilliant part, and where the real fun came in, was that all the leaders would make their sounds at the same time, and all the kids were blindfolded. The first leader to have all his/her kids reach them won the game.

As you can imagine, the scene was absolute chaos! But even more impressive was that it worked. A number of teams found their leader. And the kids had a very concrete example of what I'm going to write about today.

What those kids faced is similar to what we face every day on our journeys of faith and purpose. Things bombarding us with conflicting messages, driving us in all sorts of directions, while feeling as if we are blindfolded along the way. This thing kills purpose more often than fear and doubt and laziness combined. What these kids fought to find their direction is what we must fight to find ours as well: distraction.

In this chapter, we are going to approach the problem of distraction in a couple ways. First, we will take a look at what distraction actually is (what goes on in our brains when we are distracted). Second, we will dive into Scripture to find what things tend to distract us. Finally, we'll cover what we can do to overcome those distractions, based on the Bible and neuroscience.

What Is Distraction?

When we talk about distraction we are talking about the prevention or interruption of our attention. If you look at the origin of the word distract, it literally means to be pulled apart or to be separated.[v]

We all know what it feels like to be distracted. Our mind drifts, our eyes begin to follow something else, we lose our place in the moment. Most of these little distractions are harmless. But the danger comes when we are distracted during critical moments: a car screeching to a halt on a highway, a loved one bares their soul in conversation with us. Those are times when our eyes and mind better not drift.

Dr. Jean-Philippe Lachaux has spent his life studying distraction and attention and has a few key takeaways to teach us.[vi]

First, the primary determinant of our attention is relevance. Simply put, how much does what's happening around me actually apply to me. One of the reasons we get distracted so easily is because we've come to believe that so few things are actually important for us. The less something matters to us or for us, the harder it will be for us to pay attention to it.

It's important to note that relevance is largely based upon perception. We pay attention to things we believe matter to us and ignore the ones we believe do not apply. This is a key factor because it ties into Dr. Lachaux's next point.

For our researcher, there are 3 factors that shape our ability to pay attention (or pull us towards distraction):

- Our habits.
- Our likes/dislikes.
- Our decisions.

Habits dictate much of our unconscious brain activity. If we have a habit of looking at our phones while we are talking to another person, then it almost doesn't matter how relevant their words for us might be, we will likely pull out our phone purely out of habit.

The bad news is that we can have a habit of being distracted, so that it becomes the default activity of our brain. The good news is that we can reshape habits (and our brains in the process). We'll talk more about this later.

Second, we are more likely to pay attention to things we like and turn away from things we dislike. This seems pretty intuitive, but it can play itself out in really interesting ways. Whether you realize it or not, you have an emotional reaction to everything in your life, positive or negative. You react to strangers passing by, signs on the wall, the pitch of someone's voice – and all of these reactions get stored as emotional responses in your brain.

Your brain remembers what is "good" and "bad" and then starts to shape itself accordingly. If you really like the color blue, and a blue car speeds past you on the highway – your brain will tell your eyes and head to look at it because it remembers that to you, blue was a positive thing. In that moment, your brain doesn't care that you're driving or in the middle of a conversation. It does its best to keep you alive and happy in the only way it knows how – by shooting every "relevant" stimulation your way.

Which brings us to the third and last factor of our attention: decision. Our habits and likes each have their own part of the brain, but they can be filtered by the front of our brain, where higher thinking and decisions are made. This last piece allows us to override the systems that are in place and focus, even in the midst of a distracting environment. Decision is arguably the most important piece of the puzzle. It can both control the other factors and help us reshape them. But we'll get to that.

Distraction is a normal part of our brain processes. It's a way of keeping us aware and observant. But it can come at a steep cost, especially in the way we live our lives.

The Bible and Distraction

From what I know about the heroes of Scripture, your ability to overcome distraction will be the number one determinant of how successful you are on your path to purpose. David was distracted by pleasure. Abraham was distracted by fear. Paul was distracted by pain. We give our distractions all sorts of names, but at the end of the day, distraction is anything that pulls our attention away from God. And it can come in many forms.

We can be distracted by the worries of this life.

Mark 4:19; Luke 21:34; Matthew 6:31-34

Don't let the life you have distract you from the life you want. All of us have way too much on our plates: work commitments, family duties, church volunteering – and the list goes on and on. But that's not an excuse God will accept. In the New Testament, we see Jesus continually going off by himself, making room in his life and schedule to just be with His Father and keep his eyes on the task at hand. Don't let the urgent crowd out the important.

We can be distracted by what scares us.

Matthew 14:28-31

In Matthew 14 we read the story of Peter walking towards Jesus on the water. In my opinion, it is one of the most beautiful and most heart-breaking examples of distraction. Peter challenged his own faith by asking Jesus to call him onto the water. He stepped out, but after a few steps in he began to sink. Why is that? Because Peter started to pay attention to the *how* of his calling over the *who*. He looked at the water, the task, instead of the One who was calling Him. And when we take our eyes off the One who calls, we let fear sink our progress.

We can get distracted by our service to God.

Luke 10:38-42

Christians need to internalize this truth: *good is the enemy of great*.[vii] In Luke 10 we see Martha doing a good thing: preparing the dinner for Jesus and his disciples. We catch her in the middle of serving, fulfilling her duty. And yet, she is the one Jesus corrects. It's so easy for us to get distracted by the good things we are doing for God that we forget to actually be with God. Jesus says in verse 42, "but few things are needed – indeed only one [and] Mary has chosen what is better." When we confine ourselves to doing good things for God, we cut ourselves off from the great things He has for us.

We can get distracted by our past.

Proverbs 4:25-26; Matthew 6:34

It was during my study of Joseph that I realized where we begin has no bearing on how far we can go. And yet, so many of us remain tied to the mistakes and pains of our past. God wants your attention in the present. He wants you to "look straight ahead" because what He has for you is not behind you, but in front. History, especially personal history, has its role to play in our stories. But often, we try to live in a place we should only visit. Learn from your past and then keep going.

We can be distracted by what others want for us.

Galatians 1:10

This one is sticky. Sometimes those closest to us, the ones we love and who know us best, aren't the ones who will help us get to what's next. Paul says it so powerfully in Galatians 1:10, "Am I trying to win the approval of human beings, or of God?" You can almost hear the volume in his voice as we read this. What are we here for!? Whose opinion matters in the end? Let me answer this on his behalf: you are not here to be the person others think you should be. You are here to become the person God created you to be. No apologies. No compromises.

We can be distracted simply because we enjoy distractions.

Galatians 5:16-17; James 4:8

The gloves are off for this one. Paul doesn't hold anything back in Galatians 5 when he calls the people out: Hey, do you know why you continue to do these sins? Because you like them. We have to admit this final truth before we can appropriately address how to fix it.

Our "flesh" wants things. If we try to ignore those wants, we will lose every single time. The power of the Gospel and the Holy Spirit is not in that it makes us stop wanting bad things. Instead, the power is that we learn to want to the right things to a greater degree.

How To Fight Distraction

With the above verses and some knowledge of how our brains work as our foundation, how do we overcome the big and small distractions we face?

Engage Your Decision Power

I believe one of the unwritten spiritual disciplines is the practice of godly decision making. As we spoke about a little above, your brain has the power to override its natural tendencies through decisions. One of the reasons we don't always make the choices we want to is because we get tired. Decision fatigue sets in and we fall back into our natural tendencies. But if we want to become the people we were meant to be, and accomplish the things we were meant to accomplish – all of that begins with making a decision.

A decision to set our minds on Christ (Colossians 3). A decision that we will forgive ourselves when we become distracted, but also that we will hold ourselves to a higher standard. We will have to remake this decision every day. But as we do, both our lives and our brains will be reshaped, and the difficult will become our default.

Cultivate Your Interest In God

Why was Jesus able to remain so focused? I think Hebrews 12:2 says it perfectly, "For the joy set before him he endured the cross." Jesus wasn't caught up in the current pain. He was focused on the future glory. He had a fundamentally different stance than we do. When we are struggling in some area in our lives, we usually hear the advice "just push through it." When we "push" we are relying on our own strength and means. Jesus never pushed, he was pulled. The "joy set before him" was so strong, so clear in his mind, that it tied a rope around his waist and pulled him through the most terrible of circumstances.

We need something to pull us. A joy that lies out in front of us, pulling us through every challenge and roadblock. All of this begins by getting into God's Word. We don't need to create the joy, God already has one for us. He has an ultimate joy we will one day experience, AND a specific joy He has crafted for you to accomplish and experience on this Earth. Cultivate it by reading what He says and believing the truths He says about you. Before long, the old distractions that used to pierce you will become like arrows bouncing off a metal shield.

Develop Proactive Habits

Many of the habits we engage in are reactive. When I feel a tinge of boredom or anxiety, I begin to bite my nails. When my phone vibrates, I check to see who it is. When the alarm wakes me up, my mind begins to race through what I have to do in order to be on time to work. These are all reactive habits. We are not the ones who start the process – some outside force is (emotion, a tool, etc.). We need reactive habits because they enable us to function. But reactivity will never get us to where we truly want to be.

Proactive habits begin with the end in mind and work backwards. If I want to make myself run before work, I would proactively lay out my clothes and shoes so that they were physically in my path. If I wanted to read the Bible more consistently, I would print out a reading plan and place it in a visible location. If I wanted more time for prayer, I would schedule a block in my calendar and treat it like any other meeting. Proactive habits don't wait for the opportunity to make a good decision – they create an environment which makes the right choice easy.

In the end, distraction is a choice. Are we willing to do the work to remain focused on what God has for us, or not? Have we decided to make His Will a priority? Will we practice recognizing His voice above all others? You have the ability to make God's call on your life easier, or more difficult, to answer. The choice is yours.

What's The Difference Between God's Will, God's Plan, and God's Call?

This might sound like an ethereal question, but I promise you it's not! I'm a firm believer that the best theology is practical theology. If we can't use what we know about God to better love Him and people, then what are we arguing about?

This question was raised by one of our members at Faithspring. As they were going through one of the lessons on calling, they asked me how pursuing their purpose fit in with God's will? Around the same time, another member asked this: What if what I feel called to do isn't God's plan?

So I did what I usually do when I get difficult questions, I went straight to Scripture. What I found were dozens of statements about God's will, a few related ideas about God's plan, and another large group of verses about

God's call. I started to notice a framework – one I don't think I've ever been taught, but after I sketched it out, I knew I had to share it.

In this chapter, I'm going to explain to you the 2 parts of each: God's will, plan, and call. And after we've grappled with a few critical ideas, we'll put them all together into a single tapestry that I know you will find immensely helpful on your journey towards purpose.

God's Will – Unchanging, Commanded, Known

Of all the writers in the Bible, Paul was by far the one most obsessed with finding and communicating God's will. Across his New Testament letters, we see numerous references to God's will – what it is, how it works, and encouragement for his readers to understand it.

There are verses that are primarily encouragement about God's will, but that never explicitly say what it is: *"that you may stand firm in the will of God..." Colossians 4:12*

Other verses relate it to specific requirements (this is the will of God...):

- Be joyful, grateful and pray. 1 Thessalonians 5:16-18

- Be a living sacrifice with a renewed mind. Romans 12:1-2
- Don't be sexually immoral. 1 Thessalonians 4:3

As we continue moving our way through Scripture, it's also clear that understanding and following the will of God is an essential part of our salvation.

Not everyone who says to me, Lord Lord, will enter the kingdom of heaven, but the one who does the will of my Father... Matthew 7:21

The world is passing away...but whoever does the will of God abides forever. 1 John 2:17

There seemed to be a divide present when talking about God's will. On the one hand, God's will was unchanging. It was this powerful current which swept up everyone and everything in its path. But on the other hand, at certain points, it seemed much less overwhelming. People could disobey God's will and get away with it.

That is when the two-level framework started to come to light. I remember Pastor John Piper addressing it in one of his sermons[viii], and I've also come across it in my readings. The idea goes like this: God's will has two parts.

The first part is His unchanging will. This is what we usually think of when we talk about God's will. If you look up the definition of "will", it says "the faculty by which a person decides on and initiates action." God's will is motivated by His core goodness and immeasurable power – that makes it unquestionable, unshakable, and unchanging.

The second part is the communication of those desired outcomes – God's commands. God commands us to be good and pure and joyful because when we are, we align with His overarching good and perfect will. God's commanded (or communicated) will, as we know, can be broken. It can be ignored, refused, and disobeyed. That's because this part is not the enforcement of what God wants, but merely the sharing of what He wants.

The final important piece of God's will that we must understand is that God's will is known. He has communicated His will to us in countless ways! In addition to the verses above, we have the 10 commandments, as well as verses like 1 Timothy 2:3-4 which remind us that God's ultimate desire is for all humans to be restored in their relationship with Him.

His unchanging will is His love for creation and work to restore it. His commanded will is for humans to experience the full, holy lives He created them for. It's these two pieces which set the foundation for what comes next.

God's Plan – Overarching, Micro, Unknown

God's plan is something many Christians stress over. They constantly ask themselves: What is God's plan for my life? Are we following God's plan? Does this (some choice we want to make) fit into God's plan? In my opinion, questions are always useful. However, I think there's a better (and more Biblical) way we can go about thinking about God's plan.

If we go to the Bible, we'll see that the idea of God having a written-out plan, like a map or set of blueprints, doesn't appear very often.

- People can despise God's plan. Psalm 107:11
- Jesus' death was part of God's plan. Acts 2:22-23
- God has hope-filled plans for us. Jeremiah 29:11
- Humans have plans, but God's plans prevail. Proverbs 16:9 & 19:21

On top of that, we see another divide. Some verses explain that we have no idea what God has planned, *"no eye has seen... no ear has heard... no mind has conceived the things God has prepared" 1 Corinthians 2:9*. Still, others tell us that we have been given some insight into what God is doing: *"For now we see dimly..." 1 Corinthians 13:12*; *"I no longer call you servants, because a servant does not know his master's business. Instead, I have called you friends, for everything that I learned from my Father I have made known to you" John 15:15*.

Up to this point, it seems like God's plan is a lot like

God's unchanging will – only more mysterious. But then we get passages like Genesis 18:16-33 where Abraham's prayer literally redirects God's plan for Sodom. Or in Joshua 10, where the leader of the Israelites prayed and the sun stopped in its tracks, essentially hitting pause on God's created order.

It became clear to me that just as there were two parts to God's will, there were also two distinct parts to God's plan.

First, God has an overarching plan for the salvation and restoration of His creation. This "macro" plan includes a separate people group (Israelites, the church), a savior who forfeited his life (Jesus), and a timeline of events that end with all things glorifying God (Philippians 2:10). This plan, much like God's primary will, is unchanging. But it's only one part of the picture.

The second part is God's micro-plans, the puzzle pieces which make up His grand plan. These are smaller events which serve the grander storyline but have a degree of flexibility or freedom. When we read stories like the ones above about Abraham and Joshua, those are examples of shifts in God's micro-plans. These are incredibly important because they show us that humans can, and should, be an integral part of what God is doing.

Unlike God's will, God's plan (both parts) is largely unknown. As we continue, you'll understand why this is the case. But God has a habit of not sharing the details of His work. He has a role for us to play, but knowing less and trusting more seems to be God's preferred method of working with humans.

God's Call – Universal, Specific, Discoverable

The final piece, God's call, is by far one of the most searched for terms in modern Christianity. And for good reason, God loves calling! If you do a simple word search in the Bible for the terms "call", "called", or "calling" you'll find anywhere from 400-700 results. These include God calling both people and nature to do, or become, various things.

I've written a lot on God's calling before: what it is and how we can answer it. But here I want to approach the topic a little differently. I want to explain it in the context of God's will and God's plan. When we're speaking about God's call in a grand sense, what is it?

Right away we see a clear trend in Scripture that part of God's call is salvation:

- Called to belong to Jesus Christ. Romans 1:6
- God as our rescuer who brings salvation. Psalm 91:14-16
- The eternal life "to which we were called." 1 Timothy 6:12

This theme of God's calling is hugely present in both the

Old and New Testaments. When God calls, it is usually out of one thing, and into another. Out of trouble and into protection; out of sin and into grace; out of hopelessness and into joy.

Another fact to note, specifically about this theme, is that God's call stems from God's character. He rescues us because He is the Rescuer. He can give us peace because He is the King of Peace. There's a sense that His call is like a gift, an invitation to take or enjoy a piece of Him that wasn't available to us before. It's a humbling way to think about calling.

Next, calling takes on an even more intimate sense when God speaks directly to a single human and invites them into a specific task.

- God calls Samuel as a boy. 1 Samuel 3
- God calls Moses from the burning bush. Exodus 3
- Jesus calls the first disciples. Matthew 4:18-22

In each of these cases (and in a number of callings not mentioned here), God's calling acts as an interruption. The specific task God had for them to do was different than what they were currently doing. Their callings required some degree of sacrifice – giving up their plans, hopes, and even loved ones – in order to be fulfilled.

Let's review. God's calling, like the topics above, can also be separated into two parts. First, God's universal call to salvation and holiness. This could also be considered a calling to freedom (Galatians 5:13), out of something oppressive and into something life-giving. Second, God uses specific calls to move individuals to fulfill unique, usually time-sensitive, opportunities. God's callings are always contextual. They make sense for the time and region they are in. They might still be radical, but God didn't call Moses to build airplanes and He isn't going to call any of us to confront Pharaoh.

Since we learned that God's will is known and God's plan is unknown, what about God's call? I believe the best answer for this is that God's call is discoverable. God's call acts as an invitation, and usually, when God extends the invitation, He also gives some information. For example, the disciples didn't know everything that would happen when they began to follow Jesus. But they knew enough to take the next steps that were in front of them.

Bringing It All Together

So how do these 6 pieces all fit together? I love making things visual, so below is a drawing/chart that does just that.

What The Bible Says About Purpose

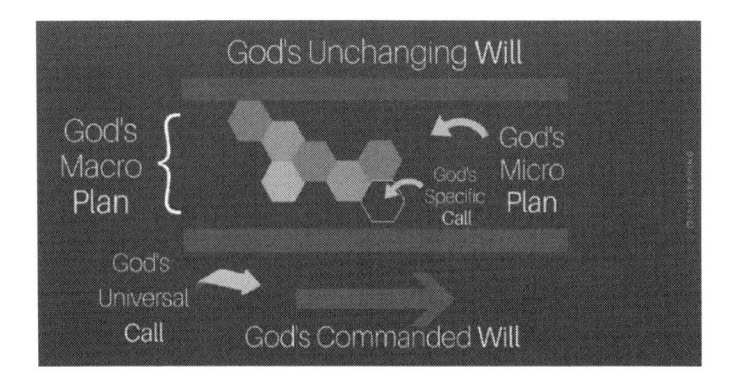

God's unchanging will is represented by the two large red lines. Think of these like street lanes or guardrails. Everything that happens – good works, sin, triumph, death, obedience, and disobedience – all occur within the boundary lines of God's unchanging will. There is nothing that can happen outside of God's allowing it.

Then how do we explain all of the evil that is present in the world? That comes under the red arrow near the bottom of the picture, which represents God's commanded will. As you can see, the arrow presents a direction to follow. Now, as we said above, this direction can be ignored or disobeyed. The arrow shows God's desired flow of events within the boundary lines of His unchanging will. As we know, people sin, which goes against God's commands, but He allows it as part of His overall unchanging will.

God's big, macro plan is represented by the blue hexagons inside God's will. These are all of the various means by which He is accomplishing His ultimate restoration. Each blue shape represents a piece of the puzzle, or God's micro plans. These could be a season in history, a movement, or even a single person. These are the pieces we have some control over. While the arrangement (macro plan) may be a mystery to us, we do know that all of it will work together for our good (*and the good of those who love God. Romans 8:28*).

Finally, we again come to the call of God which plays itself out in two parts. God's universal call is an invitation to follow God's commanded will. The call can come through many different avenues: the Holy Spirit, hearing God's Word, or being on the receiving end of God's love through people. The call invites us to do things God's way.

The specific call is similar in that it is also an invitation, this time into a piece of God's micro plan. If you look at the blank hexagon, that is God's invitation to you. Your gift and your life fit into God's grand plan in a very important way. The details and arrangement may not make sense at first, but as we seek God the path will become clearer.

Conclusion

Here's a quick summary of the 6 parts and how they each fit together:

- *Unchanging Will* – boundaries for what God allows
- *Commanded Will* – God's desired direction for creation
- *Macro Plan* – arrangement of historical events and characters
- *Micro Plan* – individual events and characters
- *Universal Call* – invitation to follow Commanded Will
- *Specific Call* – invitation to fulfill our unique role (Micro Plan)

I hope now you can understand a little bit more how the call on your life fits into God's ultimate plan for the world. Whatever the reason you are here, whatever the task you have been assigned – it's vital! How can I know that? Because you're here. You're alive and reading this. And that alone means God has something extraordinary for you to do.

Stop Waiting: A Biblical Look At God's Timing

Time is the most valuable thing a person can spend. – Theophrastus

If you're alive and Christian, chances are you've been frustrated by God's timing at some point in your life. Whether it's waiting for the right person to marry, hoping to land a new job, or praying for God's healing hand to come and do its work.

God's timing is rarely in line with our own. We struggle and pray and cross our arms, trying to do the holy thing and be patient, all the while we feel our insides beginning to boil at God's inaction. The good news is that you're not alone.

Throughout Scripture we see numerous conflicts between human impatience and divine scheduling. The question is why? Why does there seem to be such a divide between when we want things and when God wants them for us?

In this chapter we're going to answer that question, especially in the way it relates to the pursuit of your purpose. We'll tackle 3 truths about God's relationship to timing. From there, I'll show you a number of examples of good and bad waiting in the Bible, as well as examples of good and bad impatience. Finally, we'll end with some practical wisdom on what you should do in order to make God's timing work for you!

3 Truths About God's Timing

1. God has a set time for *some* things.

But when the set time had fully come, God sent his Son, born of a woman, born under the law. Galatians 4:4

He said to them: "It is not for you to know the times or dates the Father has set by his own authority. Acts 1:7

The eyes of all look to you, and you give them their food at the proper time (due season). Psalm 145:15

In the Bible, we see instances of God's unchangeable timeline. In Galatians, the writer tells us that Jesus' appearance was not by chance. God chose that age, that place, and those people very specifically.

In the big picture view of things, God has events and timelines that are non-negotiable. For example: when He began creating, when Adam breathed his first breath, when Jesus rose from the cross, and when you were born. These events were cemented into the tapestry of history.

But it's important that we realize God does not have a set time for every single thing. If I can base my theory off the Bible, it looks as though God spreads these essential events across time, and in between them are opportunities for influence as we'll see next.

2. God allows for flexibility in His timing.

For everything there is a season, and a time for every matter under heaven. Eccl 3:1

At that time Joshua spoke to the Lord..."sun stand still..." Joshua 10:12

The dead man sat up and began to talk, and Jesus gave him back to his mother. Luke 7:15

I once heard a sermon about how little we understand the power God has given us.[ix] God has invited us into the running of this universe, but so often we don't see it that way. And one of the most powerful examples of this is in how we can influence God's timing.

In Joshua 10, we dive into the middle of an intense conflict. Israel is at war and in order to win, they need daylight. Instead of complaining or retreating in fear, Joshua raises his hands and prays - asking God to stop the sun in its tracks. I'll let you read what happened next:

The sun stopped in the midst of heaven and did not hurry to set for about a whole day. There has been no day like it before or since, when the Lord heeded the voice of a man, for the Lord fought for Israel. V.13b-14

A human, Joshua, hit pause on God's natural order for the universe. Think about that. God "heeded" or paid attention to what Joshua needed, and responded in a miraculous way.

In Luke 7, we see something just as miraculous. Jesus sees a widow crying because her son has died. His time, as we would say, had run out. But because of her tears and need, Jesus *breaks* the rules. He raises the son, altering the destiny of his time upon this earth.

These are just a few examples of the theme that runs throughout both the Old and New Testaments: not every event is written in stone. We have the ability to change more than we think.

3. Waiting is an important piece of God's timing.

It is good to wait quietly. Lamentations 3:26a

If you take a minute to Google "God's timing", the first 10 pages will give you articles about waiting. Why is that? Because in the Bible, waiting is by far the most common command and response to the question of timing.

Wait for the Lord. Psalms 27:14

Be still and wait patiently. Psalms 37:7

None who wait will be put to shame. Psalms 25:3

My soul waits in silence. Psalms 62:1

Over 130 times in the Bible we are told to wait, or reminded of the benefits of waiting. It's no wonder that this has become our default stance in the modern church. When an issue or need arises, instead of running to fix or work or even pray, we wait. We wait because we believe that is the most "biblical" thing we can do.

And yes, while waiting is an important piece of God's timing – it is still only one piece. In fact, I would even say Jesus had a different "default" response for us in mind.

Examples of Good and Bad Waiting in the Bible

Waiting is a legitimate and holy practice in response to God's timing. So many verses speak about the benefits of waiting because it can transform us. It can shift our perspective, and build our muscle of trust in a way no other exercise can. Here are a few positive examples:

Joseph Waits for Freedom

Joseph, the son of Jacob, and brother to a very interesting group of guys, sits in prison for years – never knowing if or when the time would come for his release. Even after he helps the king's servants interpret their dreams, he would still have to wait another 2 years until he was called to fulfill his purpose of serving the king, and saving God's people.

Job Waits for an Answer

After his life is decimated, Job experiences a flurry of emotions. Anger, sorrow, frustration, confusion, and so much more. His friends do their best to help at first. But Job's stubbornness makes them angry, and they begin to argue, rather than comfort their friend. Job will not relent. He wants an answer from God himself, which miraculously comes at the end of the book. Job's answer was not what he expected, but it transformed the theology of Job and his friends.

Joseph, Job, and even Jesus waited. They waited because they trusted that God had something better in mind than what they could accomplish in their own power. So they humbled themselves, and allowed God to work in His own timing. But like I said before, not every wait is positive. Some are not driven by hope, but by fear.

Jacob Fears More Loss

In the later chapters of Genesis, an extreme famine hits the land. So much so, that families from across the region have to buy their food from Egypt since their land will not produce any. Jacob, the patriarch of the family, stubbornly resists sending his sons to get food. He fears losing another son – which is exactly what happens when Joseph decides to keep one of his brothers behind. Fast forward a few chapters, and everything is set right again when Jacob and Joseph reunite. But that does not make up for the danger Jacob put his family in. He waited for a miracle not from a place of hope, but from a place of fear.

Moses Fears Defeat

In Numbers 13 the nation of Israel is at a turning point. The 12 spies return from viewing the Promise Land, but the report isn't what Moses hoped. They tell stories of huge giants and massive walls. There's no way, in their minds, that they can win the battle. Even when Caleb speaks up and challenges them to trust in God, the obstacles just seem too big. Moses turns the people around and begins the wait. A wait that would last 40 years.

Waiting is not always positive, because it is not always done from a place of hope. Fear has a nasty way of disrupting and rerouting God's timing in the world. We are called to be people of faith – people who put our eyes on the promises and the Promiser above anything else. And when we don't, we can fall into a faithless, fruitless wait.

Examples of Good and Bad Impatience in the Bible

Impatience may not be the best word to use here. When I say impatience, I want you to think of *hopeful action*. Action taken with the expectation that God would also act on their behalf. Here are two examples.

Ruth Takes Action Towards Marriage

Ruth is one of my favorite Old Testament characters because she is fierce and unafraid to go after what she wants. We see this in the way she followed Naomi to her homeland. We also see this in how she humbly pursues Boaz's hand in marriage. With Naomi's guidance, Ruth makes a very risky move in chapter 3 and lays at his feet in the middle of the night. She didn't wait around and twiddle her thumbs. She went after it, took hopeful action, and God blessed her efforts.

David Takes Action Towards Victory

No one knew who David was on the day he marched into the Israelite war camp. He was there to deliver his brothers some food, but when he heard the fowl ravings of Goliath, David had to do something. So he volunteered to slay the giant. Nowhere in these verses do we see David pray about the issue, or wait for guidance. He moves, quickly and confidently, in the direction of hopeful action. And once again, God shows up and blesses the risk.

Ruth and David had no idea how their actions would turn out. They had no evidence that their risk would pay off. All they knew was that their action was based on something greater than themselves: a love for God, and a love for people. Ruth's action benefited Naomi and her deceased husband. David's action benefited all of Israel. They risked their own safety for the benefit of others and reaped great rewards.

But again, not all hopeful actions are positive. Some are also done from a place of fear and carry with them destructive consequences.

Simon Peter Rushes To Violence

Emotions are high in John 18. Jesus is in the midst of

getting arrested and Simon Peter is not going to sit idly by. He reaches for his sword and attacks the guards, cutting off one of the soldier's ears. Jesus rebukes Simon. He let his emotions get the best of him. He allowed fear to drive him and resorted to violence.

Josiah Rushes to War

By all accounts, Josiah was a good king. He was a rational man, and when he discovered the *Book of the Law* he stirred a revival in the land. He wanted to honor God, but that did not stop him from engaging in a war he could not win. Josiah went to fight Necho, king of Egypt. Different sources tell us different stories, but they all conclude the same way. This was not Josiah's fight, and he paid the ultimate price for his impatience.

Simon and Josiah both had good intentions. They wanted to save their loved ones. They wanted to be protectors and heroes, and were willing to go to whatever lengths necessary. But for God, impatience that leads to sin is never okay. The ends never justify the means. We may not be able to always tell the difference between hopeful action and fearful reaction, but God can. And He cares just as much about what motivates our actions as he does about the actions themselves.

What Should We Do

How should we respond to God's timing? Do we wait, bide our time and learn to exercise the muscle of trust? Or do we push forward, take massive action, and build the muscle of hope?

The simple answer is both. As Ecclesiastes 3 tells us, *there is a time for everything*. There's a time for risky maneuvers and there's a time for silent stillness. One is not inherently holier than the other. They each have their purpose, and they will each play their parts in the story God has for us.

But what should our *default* be? Especially when it comes to our purpose? I wholeheartedly believe that answer is hopeful action (impatience). Throughout the Gospels we see people of action:

- People rushing to Jesus to receive healing, crawling out of caves, climbing trees, and breaking through ceilings just to speak to him
- We see disciples, brand new to this life of ministry, being sent out on their own and quite literally transforming the towns they visited
- In Jesus we see the most hopeful actions of all – working tirelessly to incite the Kingdom of God, and then sacrificing His life for the coming age of glory

Jesus was a man of action. Everyone Jesus touched,

from Matthew to Mary, was driven to hopeful action because of him. And once he handed the mantle over to us, he called us to be people of action. What needs to come about in this world will not happen through waiting (Matthew 11:12).

The same goes for your story, your purpose, and your calling. What needs to happen in your life will not ultimately be fulfilled through waiting. It must come through hopeful action. If you want all that God has for you, then you must act and pray and risk and struggle.

God's timing for you will follow the three truths mentioned above: There are some things set in stone. There will be seasons of waiting. And there are large areas over which you have incredible influence and flexibility. Use them wisely. Use them to glorify God in the way you were uniquely made to.

The sad truth is that we often wait for opportunities to come that we are called to create.

God's timing is important, but it is largely outside of our knowledge and control. So what we can do, what we must do, is make the most of the time we do have knowledge of and control over. Your time of waiting is over. Consider this your permission to go.

Your Next Steps

I hope more than anything else, you will take away these two truths:

1. God cares deeply, voraciously, and jealously for your purpose.
2. Nothing will work unless you do.

Right now, you probably have a thousand ideas and questions about where to begin. Good! That means God's spirit is not only stirring your heart, but your mind – and He is already aligning things, sending opportunities, and opening doors. The beauty about being one of God's children is that for every step we take towards Him, He takes a hundred towards us.

The very next action is simple. Go here: http://www.ramosauthor.com/clarity-questions and download the free book "*5 Questions That Create Clarity.*" It's the perfect supplement to what you've discovered in this book, and will help you sift through your thousand ideas down to the ones that really matter.

After that, your next action will be to find a community. A community of people who believe in you and for you. Who will support what God has for you and will keep you accountable on the path you are on. For some, that community might come through church. For others, you may not know where to find that kind of support – and that is why Faithspring was created.

Faithspring is a membership site for ambitious Christians. Inside you'll find a vibrant community of purpose-driven believers, a collection of video courses, downloadable worksheets, recommended reading lists, and so much more. All in the service of one purpose:

To equip you to become *the who* God has called you to be

So that you can accomplish *the what* He has called you to do.

I encourage you to come, explore, and join. Because as Rick Warren says, "Nothing shapes your life more than the commitments you choose to make."

Begin your transformation here:
http://www.ramosauthor.com/clarity-questions

About the Author

David Ramos is a Christian author and Bible teacher who is passionate about communicating the life-changing truths found in Scripture. He has a B.A. in Classical and Medieval Studies (like C.S. Lewis), an M.A. in Biblical Studies from Ashland Theological Seminary, and recently completed a Certificate of Theology from Princeton Theological Seminary. His goal is to educate others so that they may serve God to greater heights by seeking Him to greater depths.

Over the last 5 years David has published over 500,000 words across nearly 100 publications and blogs. His books (12+) have reached over 100,000 readers and garnered invitations to speak at churches and universities across the country.

Learn more at RamosAuthor.com.

More Books by David Ramos

Climbing with Abraham: 30 Devotionals to Help You Grow Your Faith, Build Your Life, and Discover God's Calling

Chosen with Esther: 20 Devotionals to Awaken Your Calling, Guide Your Heart, and Empower You To Lead By God's Design

Daring with Ruth: 18 Devotionals to Ignite Your Courage, Transform Your Hope, and Reveal God's True Character

Crowned with David: 40 Devotionals to Inspire Your Life, Fuel Your Trust, and Help You Succeed in God's Way

David Ramos

Enduring with Job: 30 Devotionals to Give You Hope, Stir Your Faith, and Find God's Power in Your Pain

Escaping with Jacob: 30 Devotionals to Help You Find Your Identity, Forgive Your Past, and Walk in Your Purpose

The God with a Plan

Twentyfive: Treasures from an Unusual Millennial Life

The Shadow of Gethsemane: An Easter Poem

Future Theology: A Beginner's Guide to Thinking Biblically About Space, Technology, and the Future of Medicine

BONUS: How Trees Survive The Winter (A Guide For Growth In Difficult Times)

One of my earliest childhood memories is of my grandma and I sitting in the living room, staring at the tree outside the window. It was a younger tree, standing a proud 10 feet tall. Its branches were long and wiry. Its leaves were scattered and, instead of blocking the sun, they would make elaborate patterns across the living room floor. It made me feel small, but in a good way. The way a big hug envelops you and makes you forget about life's troubles.

Ever since then I've had a fascination with trees. If humans are a little lower than angels, I'd like to think nature is a little below us (Hebrews 2:7). And even if nature cannot talk or read or think, it can celebrate its Creator, and teach us something about life.

Like humans, nature is confined to a lifecycle. It grows,

reproduces, and eventually, dies. Nature lives in our world, is affected by the decisions we make, yet somehow survives. The tallest trees are over 300 feet tall. The oldest have stood their ground for thousands of years. They are monuments of fortitude.

As a northerner growing up near Lake Erie in Ohio, I have seen my fair share of harsh winters. Snow can pile up so high it has to be counted in feet rather than inches; and temperatures can drop so low, you'd wish negative numbers didn't exist. Yet through all the snow storms and cold bouts, trees survive.

During the past year I have spent a lot of time studying how a person grows: physically, emotionally, mentally, and spiritually. I want to understand why Christian growth is so difficult, and why it can feel like we are making no progress at times.

I believe nature, specifically trees, have something to teach us about growth. Especially growth during cold, hard seasons. There's a method to their fortitude, and hopefully one we can apply.

There are three steps every tree takes when it is faced with the seasonal change to winter. These three steps are not necessarily sequential. Instead, they work in tandem. Each one spurring on the next until the tree is as secure as it can be.

Step 1: The tree slows (or stops) growing.

The process for a tree is similar to that of an animal. Except, instead of calling it hibernation we call it *dormancy*. When a tree goes dormant that just means it has significantly slowed the process of growth. All of the food and energy it consumed are now only there for reserve and survival purposes.

Growth is an "expensive" endeavor in terms of what it requires of the living organism. If you have ever looked up the diet plans for professional athletes or bodybuilders, it's almost unbelievable how much food they have to intake in order to achieve and maintain their results.

In the same way, a tree consumes enormous amounts of energy throughout the year. However, since winter brings along less access to sunlight and water, the tree has to prepare to "eat" less and begins to slow down and hit pause on its growth.

Step 2: The tree loses its leaves.

This process only occurs in deciduous (regular, leafy) and not in coniferous (evergreen, pine needle) trees. Deciduous trees lose their leaves in order to preserve moisture and retain water. Leaves help trees grow during the year, but without the process of growth occurring, they just become a drain on the entire system.

Our bodies mimic this activity in the winter. When we are cold, our extremities (fingers and toes) will go numb first. This happens because the blood flow becomes concentrated around our vital organs. In order to protect the person, some parts have to be forfeited. Same with the tree: in order to preserve it through the winter, the beautiful leaves have to be abandoned for a time.

Step 3: The cells adapt.

There are at least three processes which could occur at the cellular level once a tree is on the verge of preparing for winter. But there are only two possible outcomes. One, the cells become more pliable (like Playdoh) so that they can adapt to the formation of icicles. Two, the cells become harder (like a rock) so that they will not be harmed by the harsh temperature and ice.

It comes down to making sure the cells stay alive: *"That's the key for the tree; don't allow living cells to freeze."* The tree will accomplish this either way it has to. Of the different processes, it doesn't appear one is better than the other because, in the end, they change back.

Without these three steps, the tree would not survive the winter. If a tree were purely concerned with growing, it would expend itself to death. In nature, there has to be a balance between longevity and growth.

Now let's take a minute and think about how these steps can apply to us as Christians.

Spiritual growth does not occur in a straight line.

The church has developed many words to characterize Christians who are not consistently experiencing victory and showing fruit. Backslider, lukewarm, etc.

But maybe these episodes are not hindrances to the process of growth but necessary milestones. I know in my own life there have been a number of times where I have fallen into a rough patch only to catapult forward afterward.

Sometimes growth can be dangerous. If a human grows too quickly, or too much, it puts so much stress on their body that serious complications can arise. Just because we cannot see our spirits does not mean they do not have their own limitations as well.

I believe growth comes in seasons. There are times where we sprout up and out and stretch ourselves without hindrance. Then there are other seasons where growth is difficult, or even non-existent. And we are forced to shrink back, to conserve energy, and pause so that growth may start again.

Christian growth can be summarized in a single word: surrender.

I began tithing when I was very young. About 5 or 6. My allowance at the time was $5 a week. I was told, by my parents and pastors, that 10% of my money belongs to God. So I believed them, and gladly gave my tithe to the church. Over time, as my allowance turned into a salary, I continued to tithe. It wasn't really a sacrifice in my mind because I was simply giving to God what was already His.

But then I started to grow up and God began to ask for more than just my 10%. I felt called into certain ministries. I felt called to leave jobs, schools, relationships and follow Him. I started to feel that God was overstepping His bounds. He was not only asking for what was His. Now, He was asking for what was clearly mine! My love life, my ambitions, my plans...these were my leaves.

In order to become *who* I was supposed to be and in order to "preserve" my life according to His purpose, He asked me to surrender. I don't believe trees can feel pain, but if they did I imagine they would feel each leaf as it fell. Like a pluck or a pinch. Each one a reminder that surrendering to something greater comes at a cost.

Life will either make us pliable or hard.

I recently took a cooking class and they explained the art of making bread from scratch. As part of the process, we learned to knead the dough, which is essentially massaging it (breaking it down) to a certain point until its ready to bake and will rise correctly.

If the dough is under-kneaded, the dough will be too fragile. Yes, it will be pliable, but it will tear easily and be too weak to rise as needed. If the dough is over-kneaded, it will become hard and too stiff to take the proper shape. The perfect spot is somewhere in the middle, where it is kneaded just enough to hold up. Pliable enough to accept change, but hard enough to not be torn.

God allows life to knead us. To break us down before He can call us to rise. The question is how will we adapt? Will we become too hard or too soft? Or will we accept the kneading process as necessary to our survival and His glory?

Trees survive the winter because they have too. If they do not survive the harsh seasons, they will never reach the points where they can grow and bear fruit. But how they survive those periods looks drastically different then when they are green and bearing fruit.

I don't know what your life or walk with God looks like at this moment, but I want to encourage you. If your leaves have fallen, that doesn't mean they will never sprout again. Maybe you've pulled back from ministry commitments, switched churches, or have experienced a drought in your prayer life. None of these make you a bad Christian. None of these make you weaker or less loved by God.

They make you human.

They make you a work in progress.

They mean you're growing.

Sources:

How do trees survive in the winter?[x]
Mother Nature Network[xi]
Northern Woodlands[xii]

BONUS: The 10 Best Articles On The Web For Finding Your Purpose

Discovering your purpose or calling can be difficult, but finding resources that can help you shouldn't be. Here are 10 of the best posts on the web that have actually helped me on my journey towards calling, and I believe they will help you as well.

You can find links to all of the mentioned articles here: http://www.faithspring.org/10-best-articles-finding-purpose/

Title: The Inciting Incident in Your Quest for Calling

Favorite line: *If the choice is between Netflix and hard work, there has to be a reason to choose the work.*

Main idea: Everyone who is pursuing their purpose seriously has experienced an "inciting incident." Something so extraordinary or painful or (rarely) good, that you had no other choice but to take yourself and your desires seriously.

The author of this article lists 9 commons moments most people encounter before they make a real change in their direction. I know personally, I've encountered about 4 of these. Reflecting on those times in my life, and remembering how my life has changed because of those moments, was truly inspiring. They reminded me that so often the place we fear to go is the place we need to go.

Title: How To Discern Your Calling

Favorite Line: *They think they need to hear an audible voice from God or there is something mystical about it. I don't think so.*

Main Idea: I love the way Michael Hyatt breaks things down. He's such a clear thinker, and he helps so many others gain clarity as well. In this article/podcast episode he provides 2 extremely useful frameworks. First, he describes calling as having four attributes:

1. External
2. Personal
3. Appealing
4. Optional (interesting word choice!)

Second, he places calling within three necessary components:

1. Passion
2. Proficiency
3. Profitability

This framework has raised a lot of interesting questions (as well as some pushback). This is one resource you won't want to skip.

Title: 4 Things Keeping You From Finding Your Purpose in Life

Favorite Line: *Take a deep breath and give yourself the grace and space to fail, without calling yourself a failure.*

Main Idea: Paul Angone was one of the first people I stumbled upon online when I started to take my own calling more seriously. I watched as he set an example for other coming-of-age millennials to take the road less traveled. I trust his writing because he's lived it. In this article, the 4 roadblocks he lists are:

1. Lack of Intentionality
2. Fear Crushing Your Confidence
3. Not Understanding Your Why
4. Lack of Community

I'm still a work in progress as far as these roadblocks are concerned. But I think that is also kind of the point. Just because a roadblock is in your way, doesn't mean your journey is over. It's part of your journey. As Ryan

Holiday would say, the obstacle is the way. Don't avoid the hard questions or uncomfortable situations, lean into them. That's where the beauty is. That's where the transformation lies.

Title: Why Having Purpose is the Secret to a Longer, Healthier Life

Favorite Line: *Thought is good, but purpose is the result of practice.*

Main Idea: When I first stumbled upon this article, I was a little lost. Sports analogies aren't exactly my thing. But as I kept reading I saw the absolute gold that was lying in wait. Clear's main point is that purpose is quite literally a life-extender. People who wake up with a reason to live, keep waking up. Sometimes for decades longer than their peers.

This article has a handful of great research links, such as the American physician who wrote a book on being old in America and the WHO statistics which show the power of the Japanese *ikigai* philosophy. The article finally ends with a call to practice – which is the route by which (as the author believes) we discover our purpose. I love anything that pairs mastery with calling because I believe they are so inextricably linked.

Title: The Complicated But Beautiful Process of Finding Your Calling

Favorite Line: *Discovery happens in stages and clarity will come with action.*

Main Idea: How do I get from here (place of uncertainty, frustration, stuckness) to there (place of purpose, calling, success)? This is a question I found myself asking a lot, especially over the last few years. I just wanted to see the path. I wanted a guide, a fairy godmother, anything. I would have taken anyone's advice so long as they could guarantee me that I was heading in the right direction.

But that's where the problem was. Jeff Goins writes an excellent article on how to get the clarity you want, without actually having to wait for the clarity you want. The key is action. Taking the next step. Putting one foot in front of the other and allowing the road to unfold as it will. "Purpose is more of a path than a plan."

This post ends with 3 great insights (you'll want to read how he expands upon these):

1. You can't do this on your own
2. You'll have to practice
3. You won't just know

Title: A stupid lie I believed when I quit my last job. (And why you shouldn't believe it.)

Favorite Line: *"Do what you love and you'll never work a day in your life" is not true, but something even better is.*

Main Idea: Fast-food never looks the way it does on television. Not once have I ever ordered a Big Mac and not had it look like a baby elephant rolled over it somewhere in between it being assembled and served to my drive-thru window.

A similar encounter happens when it comes to living out our purpose. There's an idea we have in our minds of what it will look and feel like. A commercial we play in our minds; one that, whether we know it or not, has been influenced by movies, social media, and the random success story we stumble across. But real purpose, like everything else of value, requires real work. Long exhausting days, confusion, running into walls, and discovering that, no, everyone doesn't like what you've created or stand for.

It can be a lot. But for those of us who feel truly called, there is no other choice. We accept the work because the alternative is unthinkable.

Title: How to Find & Do Work You Love

Favorite Line: *The only thing that limits possibility is imagination.*

Main Idea: We must not be afraid to create our own definition of success. It's something we hear a lot: don't compare your chapter 1 to someone else's chapter 20, stay in your lane, focus on what you really want. But it's so hard not to want to measure our success and progress on some kind of standard like how much money are we making, how many people are we impacting, and so on.

The author of this talk challenges us to not fall into that trap. With example after example, Scott Dinsmore proves those who have had the biggest impact in this world, and who have lived the most satisfying lives, did so by defining their own idea of success and then unapologetically pursuing it.

This talk provides a number of useful tools such as how our unique strengths, experiences, and values work together to illuminate what we really want. Also, you can see the foundation of his 4-part framework:

1. Become a self-expert
2. Do your impossible
3. Surround yourself with a passionate community
4. Do something that matters

Title: Stop Waiting For God To Tell You What To Do With Your Life

Favorite Line: *He believed that if he was patient enough, eventually God would reveal his true calling. I told him I don't think God works like that.*

Main Idea: Waiting sucks. Pretty much every human alive hates waiting. If you're looking for a good business to start, just look for a way to cut down people's wait times in some area (fast food, instant streaming, other).

Now, even though we hate waiting so much, sometimes we will use it as an excuse. "I'm waiting on God" or "I'm waiting for the right time." What's strong enough to make us change our feelings about waiting: fear.

Justin Zoradi cuts through the fog and lays it out beautifully. So many of us hold back from fulfilling our calling because we're afraid. Afraid to risk, afraid to commit to an idea, afraid to get caught being our true selves. But that's the only option, to confront the fear and abandon the wait. "God joins us only [after] we take that initial risk."

Title: How To Differentiate Passion From Calling

Favorite Line: *Don't let what you want to do prevent what you're meant to do.*

Main Idea: As Jim Collins has said, "Good is the enemy

of great." Dale Partridge delivers an intimate look into how pursuing your purpose requires more than just seizing every opportunity that crosses your path.

I know I have fallen into the habit and saying yes too quickly and too often. But so often, our calling does not lie on the other side of a hundred yeses. Rather, it requires a series of strategic nos.

Dale provides 3 truths that must fit the opportunity before we can say yes (and to help us say no).

1. It should support our greater calling, not detract from it
2. Just because it's smart doesn't mean its right (good vs. great)
3. Good decisions don't happen alone

Title: Finding Your Calling Part IV: Discovering Your Vocation

Favorite Line: *Finding your true vocation means finding work that utilizes your gifts in the 75-100% range.*

Main Idea: I absolutely love how practical this article makes the idea of finding our calling. This one from Brett McKay is the 4th part of a 5 part series on vocation (aka the work you were meant to do). As you can see from my favorite line above, the author believes there's a formula to finding our best fit. The reason some places might feel "almost right" is because, in some important ways, they might be. But until we get closer to that sweet spot, where the majority of our time and effort is spent on what we are particularly good at and want to do, we'll always feel like something is off.

His formula is: True Vocation = Your Gifts + Your Passion.

By gifts, he means our "birthright gifts" which are talents or abilities which come naturally to us (whether we've discovered them yet or not). For passion, he uses the idea of an inner signal. We must rediscover our internal cues, and stop being driven by external cues.

I would recommend reading the entire 5 part series, but definitely start here.

BONUS: Every Verse About Purpose In The Bible

Exodus 9:16

But I have raised you up for this very purpose, that I might show you my power and that my name might be proclaimed in all the earth.

Leviticus 7:24

The fat of an animal found dead or torn by wild animals may be used for any other purpose, but you must not eat it.

1 Chronicles 23:5

Four thousand are to be gatekeepers and four thousand are to praise the Lord with the musical instruments I have provided for that purpose.

Job 36:5

God is mighty, but despises no one; he is mighty, and firm in his purpose.

Job 42:2

I know that you can do all things; no purpose of yours can be thwarted.

Psalm 33:10

The Lord foils the plans of the nations; he thwarts the purposes of the peoples.

Psalm 33:11

But the plans of the Lord stand firm forever, the purposes of his heart through all generations.

Proverbs 19:21

Many are the plans in a person's heart, but it is the

Lord's purpose that prevails.

Proverbs 20:5

The purposes of a person's heart are deep waters, but one who has insight draws them out.

Isaiah 10:7

But this is not what he intends, this is not what he has in mind; his purpose is to destroy, to put an end to many nations.

Isaiah 14:24

The Lord Almighty has sworn, "Surely, as I have planned, so it will be, and as I have purposed, so it will happen."

Isaiah 14:27

For the Lord Almighty has purposed, and who can thwart him? His hand is stretched out, and who can turn it back?

Isaiah 46:10

I make known the end from the beginning, from ancient times, what is still to come. I say, 'My purpose will stand, and I will do all that I please.'

Isaiah 46:11

From the east I summon a bird of prey; from a far-off land, a man to fulfill my purpose. What I have said, that I will bring about; what I have planned, that I will do.

Isaiah 48:14

"Come together, all of you, and listen: Which of the idols has foretold these things? The Lord's chosen ally will carry out his purpose against Babylon; his arm will be against the Babylonians."

Isaiah 55:11

So is my word that goes out from my mouth: It will not return to me empty, but will accomplish what I desire and achieve the purpose for which I sent it.

Jeremiah 15:11

The Lord said, "Surely I will deliver you for a good purpose; surely I will make your enemies plead with you in times of disaster and times of distress."

Jeremiah 23:20

The anger of the Lord will not turn back until he fully accomplishes the purposes of his heart. In days to come you will understand it clearly.

Jeremiah 30:24

The fierce anger of the Lord will not turn back until he fully accomplishes the purposes of his heart. In days to come you will understand this.

Jeremiah 32:19

Great are your purposes and mighty are your deeds. Your eyes are open to the ways of all mankind; you reward each person according to their conduct and as their deeds deserve.

Jeremiah 49:20

Therefore, hear what the Lord has planned against

Edom, what he has purposed against those who live in Teman: The young of the flock will be dragged away; their pasture will be appalled at their fate.

Jeremiah 50:45

Therefore, hear what the Lord has planned against Babylon, what he has purposed against the land of the Babylonians: The young of the flock will be dragged away; their pasture will be appalled at their fate.

Jeremiah 51:11

"Sharpen the arrows, take up the shields! The Lord has stirred up the kings of the Medes, because his purpose is to destroy Babylon. The Lord will take vengeance, vengeance for his temple."

Jeremiah 51:12

Lift up a banner against the walls of Babylon! Reinforce the guard, station the watchmen, prepare an ambush! The Lord will carry out his purpose, his decree against the people of Babylon.

Jeremiah 51:29

The land trembles and writhes, for the Lord's purposes against Babylon stand— to lay waste the land of Babylon so that no one will live there.

Luke 7:30

But the Pharisees and the experts in the law rejected God's purpose for themselves, because they had not been baptized by John.

Acts 5:38

Therefore, in the present case I advise you: Leave these men alone! Let them go! For if their purpose or activity is of human origin, it will fail.

Acts 13:36

"Now when David had served God's purpose in his own generation, he fell asleep; he was buried with his ancestors and his body decayed."

Romans 8:28

And we know that in all things God works for the good of those who love him, who have been called according to his purpose.

Romans 9:11

Yet, before the twins were born or had done anything good or bad—in order that God's purpose in election might stand

Romans 9:17

For Scripture says to Pharaoh: "I raised you up for this very purpose, that I might display my power in you and that my name might be proclaimed in all the earth."

Romans 9:21

Does not the potter have the right to make out of the same lump of clay some pottery for special purposes and some for common use?

1 Corinthians 3:8

The one who plants and the one who waters have one purpose, and they will each be rewarded according to their own labor.

2 Corinthians 5:5

Now the one who has fashioned us for this very purpose is God, who has given us the Spirit as a deposit, guaranteeing what is to come.

Galatians 4:18

It is fine to be zealous, provided the purpose is good, and to be so always, not just when I am with you.

Ephesians 1:9

He made known to us the mystery of his will according to his good pleasure, which he purposed in Christ

Ephesians 1:11

In him we were also chosen, having been predestined according to the plan of him who works out everything in conformity with the purpose of his will

Ephesians 2:15

By setting aside in his flesh the law with its commands

and regulations. His purpose was to create in himself one new humanity out of the two, thus making peace

Ephesians 3:11

According to his eternal purpose that he accomplished in Christ Jesus our Lord.

Ephesians 6:22

I am sending him to you for this very purpose, that you may know how we are, and that he may encourage you.

Philippians 2:13

For it is God who works in you to will and to act in order to fulfill his good purpose.

Colossians 4:8

I am sending him to you for the express purpose that you may know about our circumstances and that he may encourage your hearts.

1 Timothy 2:7

And for this purpose I was appointed a herald and an apostle—I am telling the truth, I am not lying—and a true and faithful teacher of the Gentiles.

2 Timothy 1:9

He has saved us and called us to a holy life—not because of anything we have done but because of his own purpose and grace. This grace was given us in Christ Jesus before the beginning of time

2 Timothy 2:20

In a large house there are articles not only of gold and silver, but also of wood and clay; some are for special purposes and some for common use.

2 Timothy 2:21

Those who cleanse themselves from the latter will be instruments for special purposes, made holy, useful to the Master and prepared to do any good work.

2 Timothy 3:10

You, however, know all about my teaching, my way of

life, my purpose, faith, patience, love, endurance

Hebrews 6:17

Because God wanted to make the unchanging nature of his purpose very clear to the heirs of what was promised, he confirmed it with an oath.

Revelation 17:13

They have one purpose and will give their power and authority to the beast.

Revelation 17:17

For God has put it into their hearts to accomplish his purpose by agreeing to hand over to the beast their royal authority, until God's words are fulfilled.

This list is from the NIV version, which contains 52 references to the word purpose. Two are in the title and introductions to Scripture, so they were not included in this list.

The ESV version contains an additional 25 references (77 total) to the word purpose, but many of these are simply a translation choice.

The MSG contains the fewest amount of references, 34 total.

[i] Definition of "consistency" from Merriam-Webster. https://www.merriam-webster.com/dictionary/consistency
[ii] Definition of "purpose" from Merriam-Webster. https://www.merriam-webster.com/dictionary/purpose
[iii] Bible Hub and Strong's Concordance findings: http://biblehub.net/searchgreek.php?q=purpose
[iv] Bible Hub and Strong's Concordance findings: http://biblehub.net/searchhebrew.php?q=purpose
[v] Online Etymology Dictionary: https://www.etymonline.com/word/distraction
[vi] Attention, distraction and the war in our brain: Jean-Philippe Lachaux at TEDxEMLYON: https://www.youtube.com/watch?v=PNbR_nbfK9c
[vii] Quote by Jim Collins: https://www.goodreads.com/quotes/701885-good-is-the-enemy-of-great-and-that-is-one
[viii] What Is the Will of God and How Do We Know It?: https://www.desiringgod.org/messages/what-is-the-will-of-god-and-how-do-we-know-it
[ix] Prayer Causes Things To Happen by John Piper (relevant portion begins at 2:45): https://youtu.be/krzwmhDMvv8?t=2m45s
[x] Article by Michigan State University, Bill Cook: http://msue.anr.msu.edu/news/how_do_trees_survive_in_the_winter
[xi] Article by Eileen Campbell: https://www.mnn.com/earth-matters/wilderness-resources/stories/how-do-trees-survive-winter
[xii] Article by Michael Snyder: http://northernwoodlands.org/outside_story/article/trees-survive-winter-cold

Made in the USA
Columbia, SC
06 May 2018